Ayr United at War

Ayr United at War

Duncan Carmichael

Mansion Field

Mansion Field
An imprint of Zeticula Ltd
The Roan,
Kilkerran,
KA19 8LS
Scotland

http://www.mansionfield.co.uk

First published in 2014
Text © Duncan Carmichael 2014
Photographs on pages ii, 24, 102 and 200 © David Carmichael.
Photograph on page 23 from the Denholm Reid collection.
Photographs on pages 26, 49, 56, 60, 148, 158 and 165 from
    the John Davie collection.
Photographs on pages 32, 36, 40, 42 and 99 by courtesy
    of the *Ayrshire Post*.
Photograph on page 90 © Roy Hay.
Caricature on page 94 © Ayr United Supporters' Association.
Caricatures on pages 96 and 127 courtesy of the *Daily Record*.
Photograph on page 174 courtesy of the family of Norrie McNeil.
Photograph on page 176 courtesy of Andy Connell.
Photograph on page 177 © Michael Green.
Some photographs which are of poor reproductive quality have nevertheless been included for their rarity and historical interest.
Every effort has been made to trace the owners of the copyright for the photographs on pages 38, 82, 112 and 156. The editor and publisher will be pleased to correct any oversights in future printings.
All rights reserved. No part of this publication may be reproduced, stored in a retrieval system, or transmitted in any form or by any means, electronic, mechanical, photocopying, recording or otherwise, without the prior permission of the publishers.

ISBN 978-1-905021-12 3

This book is dedicated to the memory of:

Private Gabriel Baird Carmichael

My great uncle, who died on 25th October, 1918, from wounds received in battle. He served in the 2nd Battalion of the Argyll and Sutherland Highlanders and paid the supreme sacrifice at the age of twenty-five, just seventeen days before the armistice.

Private David Porteous

My great uncle, who died at the age of twenty-eight, on 18th November, 1916. He was killed at the battle of Beaumont-Hamel on that date. His unit was the 17th Battalion of the Highland Light Infantry.

Private James Marshall Boning

The grandfather of my wife Carol. At the age of twenty he was discharged from the Highland Light Infantry on 14th January, 1917, after having a leg amputated.

The Fallen of Ayr FC, Parkhouse and Ayr United

Corporal John Bellringer – Ayr United. 'C'Company. 1st/5th Battalion Argyll and Sutherland Highlanders. Died at Gallipoli at the age of 23 on 12th July, 1915.

Private Samuel Herbertson – Ayr United. 1st/4th Battalion Royal Scots Fusiliers. Died at Gallipoli at the age of 26 on 12th July, 1915.

Private Robert Capperauld – Ayr United. 5th Battalion Royal Scots Fusiliers. Died on 14th July, 1915, after suffering wounds at Gallipoli.

Private Thomas Clifford – Ayr FC. 6th/7th Battalion Royal Scots Fusiliers. Died at the Somme at the age of 42 on 19th January, 1917.

Private Hugh Kerr – Ayr FC. 14th Battalion London Scottish. Died at the Western Front on 10th April, 1918.

2nd Lieutenant William Kerr – Parkhouse. Machine Gun Corps 4th Battalion Royal Scots Fusiliers. Died at the Western Front at the age of 37 on 2nd September, 1918.

Archie Campbell – Ayr United. 119th Brigade Royal Field Artillery. Died of war wounds at the age of 38 on 14th September, 1918.

James Croall – Parkhouse. Civilian. Drowned near Yeovil at the age of 54. Body discovered on 18th September, 1939, after he had been missing for a week.

Acknowledgements

In collating the images for this book it was necessary to explore beyond those in my personal collection. In pursuit of that end I remain most grateful to Denholm Reid for providing a century-old photograph of Somerset Road. It simply oozes social history. Fix that image in your mind and you will have a clear picture of what the enthusiasts (as fans were then known) saw on their approach to Somerset Park. You can take it for granted that the street was more heavily populated on match days.

Of equal fascination is the photograph of David Beckham and Michael Green holding an Ayr United scarf aloft. I thank Michael for his kind permission to use this image. With an apology for resorting to a cliché it really has to be said that you could not make it up.

Andy Connell, I thank you for a photographic contribution too. The message is clear. You really could have been somewhere worse than Afghanistan. It is incumbent upon the reader to decide whether or not you were joking.

The photography theme will be laboured a little more to thank my son David for getting behind the lens to snap some of the illustrations contained within. His fee was a roll and sausage. Honestly, it was! My wife Carol and daughter Jill must also be thanked for their patience whilst another book was being worked on.

I extend gratitude to Colm Hickey for supporting material on Lawrence Gemson. Colm wrote an excellent article on Mr Gemson in the *Catholic Life* magazine and he permitted me to use some details from it.

To Roy Hay, grandson of Jimmy Hay, I am indebted for the illustration of the great man's medal. I am equally indebted to John Davie for access to his superb collection of photographs and cigarette cards.

The ladies who helped me to access records in the local history department of Ayr's Carnegie Library were most co-operative and courteous and I wish to express my thanks for that.

Most of all I am grateful for the inspiration drawn from the spirit of Ayr United Football Club. Notwithstanding the point that people will die, the spirit of the club will live on.

Duncan Carmichael
Monkton, February 2014.

Contents

The Fallen of Ayr FC, Parkhouse and Ayr United   vii

Acknowledgements   ix

List of Illustrations   xiii

Introduction   xv

1. The Boer War   1

2. The Great War   22

3. Some Characters of the Great War   131

4. The Second World War   144

5. Afghanistan   175

Fixtures   179
    Ayr FC's record during the Boer War   180
        1899/00   180
        1900/01   182
        1901/02   184
    Ayr United 1914/15   186
        1915/16   188
        1916/17   190
        1917/18   192
        1918/19   194
        1939/40 - first start   196
        1939/40 Regional League   198

Index   201

List of Illustrations

For Your Tomorrow	*ii*
This image was taken right outside Somerset Park. It is from a postcard sent on 4th February, 1914.	*23*
The view in February 2014.	*24*
Johnny Crosbie - The club agreed to pay him half wages while on military service.	*26*
Army recruitment drive at the Ayr United versus Morton match on 14th November, 1914.	*32*
Alec Gray scoring in a 2-1 win over Aberdeen on 18th April, 1914.	*36*
Jack Lyall - He was a showman in an age in which goalkeepers were seldom inclined to display flamboyancy.	*38*
On 15th August, 1914. In searing heat Ayr United beat Partick Thistle 4-0 at Somerset Park. Beforehand the team posed for the camera	*40*
Jimmy Richardson scoring in a 2-0 victory at home to Rangers on 17th October, 1914.	*42*
Willie McStay - Loaned from Celtic from November 1912 until the summer of 1916.	*49*
Hilly (Alex Hill) Goodwin. He survived active service in the Great War and lived until the age of fifty-seven.	*56*
Switcher McLaughlan - His trade absented him from the call of the Great War.	*60*
George Waddell - He gave sterling war time service to Ayr United after ignoring Kilmarnock's enquiry.	*82*
The campaign medal of Gunner Hay.	*90*
Neil McBain, an outstanding Ayr United player and, eventually, manager.	*94*
George Nisbet - His fearlessness in the Ayr United goal would indicate that he was an asset in the trenches.	*96*

Billy Middleton - Wounded in action, patched up then wounded again.	99
Ayr Cemetery contains a beautiful commemoration to the Newfoundlanders.	102
John Cameron - His war resembled fiction.	112
Jimmy Richardson - Still not recovered from a stomach wound suffered in trench warfare he returned to score a glorious hat-trick.	127
Terry McGibbons - The outbreak of the Second World War brought a premature end to his senior career.	148
Frank Thompson - The Ayr United manager when the club ceased for the duration of World War Two.	156
James 'Henry' Hall - Custodian of the Ayr United goal at the outbreak of World War Two.	158
Andy McCall - He returned to Ayr United briefly in 1940.	165
Norrie McNeil became a rock at the heart of the Ayr United defence.	174
Andy Connell	176
David Beckham and Michael Green	177
In lesser and better known conflicts they fell.	200

Introduction

"There's famine in Africa. That puts Ayr United's relegation troubles into perspective." This typifies the time honoured response of philosophical supporters when the fortunes of the club are foundering. The retort is prone to variation. It is incumbent on the individual to mention the global catastrophe of choice. Whatever the version it raises the same central issue. That issue is perspective. Drearily we are left to contemplate the notion that any woes perpetrated at Somerset Park are miniscule in comparison to the more potent issue of human suffering in the wider world. On the basis of logic it is not open to question that this is true. Yet logic can be a rare ingredient in the morass of emotions experienced by those fans who are disinclined towards philosophical traits or utterances.

The enduring nature of local football has allowed it to survive the most appalling global conflicts and economic upheaval. A prime example is the Great War. Amidst the grief, shortages and general difficulties visited upon people it might reasonably be assumed that the Somerset Park regulars were more temperate in their support of Ayr United. That would be a wayward assumption. In September 1916 the board felt compelled to make a public statement threatening bans on those guilty of unruly behaviour. The hooligans, by their actions, were not in the least constrained by the news of slaughter on the battlefields of the Somme. It was ultimate proof of the game's tendency to transcend almost anything. As a side note it might further be observed that it was equal proof that banning orders, or the threat of them, was not a deterrent devised in modern times.

Old Lady Somerset has witnessed deeply respectful tributes to tragedy. In 1901 the players wore black armbands out of respect for the recently departed Queen Victoria. In 2001 a minute's silence was held for the victims of 9/11. On both occasions the visiting club was St. Mirren. Did the sombre mood have a detrimental effect on the players and spectators once the action was underway? From personal recollection it can be recorded here that passions were not unduly disturbed in 2001. Neither is there documentary evidence to suggest that it was any different one hundred years earlier. Football's propensity to shrug it all off may be unprincipled but it is ingrained in the game regardless of the moral view taken. The balance may be redressed a little. In times of conflict the board of Ayr United has been quick to implement charitable gestures. The provision of complimentary tea to wounded Tommies was one such example. Or rather it was until such time as the scarcity of sugar caused the gesture to be withdrawn.

To describe relegation as a tragedy is a clichéd response. The story about to unfold will relate much tragedy in a true rather than a metaphorical context.

1.

The Boer War

 Territorial disputes are a common cause of escalation into a war. The minute detail of the cause of the Boer War is beyond the remit of this book but, to put it concisely, the Boers were Dutch settlers in South Africa and it was considered that the lands being farmed by them railed against British sovereignty. The war began at 5 p.m. on Wednesday, 11th October, 1899. That was the expiry time by which the Boers required an immediate and affirmative answer to their ultimatum. Ultimatum is a seemingly unavoidable word in relation to the origin of war. This one had not the remotest glimmer of achieving conciliation. It required the withdrawal of British troops from the neighbourhood of the Transvaal borders. The clock chimed five and from that moment a state of war existed between Her Majesty's Government and the Republics of the Transvaal and the Orange Free State. In more simplified terms it was British and Empire troops versus Dutch farmers. The opposition had the mandatory hate figure upon whom the people of Britain could express revulsion. That man was Paul Kruger, the president of the Transvaal.

 Thus far we have the mandatory ultimatum, the mandatory grievance and the mandatory villain. To this we may add the mandatory "all over by Christmas" prophecies. The columns of the *Ayr Observer* hinted that the fighting would last a little longer. When the declaration was imminent it was stated: "It would be a mistake to conclude that if we have to unsheathe the sword in the Transvaal it will be a quick and easy walk over. It may extend over a good many months." The anonymous writer at least foresaw it extending beyond Christmas, although his prophecy was equated in months rather than years. It took until 31st May, 1902, for the peace treaty to be signed.

Of course Ayr United did not stalk the land in 1899, a fact that is rather contradictory of the book title. We are now in the realms of the club's family tree. Ayr FC, based at Somerset Park, and Parkhouse, based at Beresford Park, were the local clubs back then and this examination will centre on the impact created on them by that faraway conflict.

On Saturday, 7th October, Ayr FC defeated Hamilton Accies 2-1 at Somerset Park. By virtue of this result the club leap-frogged Hamilton Accies to attain second bottom place in the Second Division. On the same day a proclamation was issued to call up the Army Reserve for service with the colours in South Africa. It was a seemingly inconsequential consideration that war had not yet been declared. Willie Massie, signed from Partick Thistle, scored just two minutes into his Ayr debut against Hamilton Accies. His son Alex was destined to become an Ayr United player in September 1925. Alas, Ayr United failed to spot the potential in Alex Massie. Perhaps it had not been apparent. He was transferred to Bury in January 1927 and went on to make a major impact with Hearts and Aston Villa whilst attaining the Scotland captaincy. This is a tenuous comparison to illustrate that football and international affairs possess an equal propensity to lack the gift of prophecy.

In Ayr and surrounds the call to the colours was quick to generate a response: "The military fervour and enthusiasm is increasing amongst our Yeomanry and Volunteers. Ayrshire's response to the call is going to be no half-hearted one, the men who are volunteering for service in South Africa being not only willing but anxious to go to the front." Colonel Jackson, secretary of the Ayr Soldiers and Sailors Association, pledged to give all possible help to the wives and families of the serving soldiers.

For each send-off Ayr Station was packed with people. Yet the farewells were possessed of a level of enthusiasm that was less than total and they pitched up short of the excitement generated when either Ayr FC or Parkhouse were playing Kilmarnock. This is borne out by the testimony of an eye-witness: "Very considerable interest was manifested in the dispatch of our gallant Reserves last week. On each occasion the station was thronged but while everyone present must have been patriotically breathing a prayer for the safe return after a brilliant victory of our brave defenders, the send-off could not be characterised as overwhelmingly enthusiastic. No, Ayr folk cannot enthuse aright [sic] – except perhaps when one of their teams chance to play Kilmarnock, then it comes away all right."

Graphic accounts of the fighting soon appeared in columns alongside the local football reports. These accounts were tinged with jingoism and were heavy in propaganda. Tales of derring-do were lyrical to the point of poetic. On the domestic front people read about Boer atrocities on women and children. "Undisciplined and ignorant Boers" were supposedly wrecking gold mines. Boer defeats were crushing. British victories were brilliant. "The Transvaal Boers have shown themselves to be at the bottom of the veriest savages" opined one of the tightly packed columns of the *Ayr Observer*.

The opportunity to cross refer football to the war was too good to resist. "On Saturday afternoon a fierce engagement took place at Elandslaagte and after most determined resistance the Boers were routed. On the same afternoon another engagement took place on Somerset Park, when the Thistle were routed with heavy loss. The Ayr force is intact."

The expression "Ayr Force" is worth closer scrutiny. Future generations would see it used as a slick play on words in favourable description of Ayr United. The obvious connotation is that of aerial flight. In 1899 aerial flight was still in the domain of experimentation by eccentrics. ELEVEN VCs WON declared a headline above a report of Ayr FC 2

Partick Thistle 1 in the same newspaper. It could have been implied that this was war without the bullets.

There was a popular line of thought that footballers should have been putting themselves in contention for a real rather than a metaphorical Victoria Cross.

"FOOTBALLERS FOR THE FRONT: There they are – sound, strong, plucky, quick in resource; in fact the very material Lord Roberts would desire to command. Men, men, men! Is the cry from South Africa, only second in importance to Horses, horses, horses!"

It is a curious notion that man was considered of secondary importance alongside a horse.

With no seeming intent at irony the *Ayr Observer* carried the following message under a headline of THE COMPLIMENTS OF THE SEASON.

"It will not to any great extent be a Merry Christmas this year. A local epidemic has laid low about 150 in our community, and a war which has already cost many lives, will very much subdue the usual exuberant good wishes and compliments which characterise this season both locally and nationally."

The mood manifested itself in connection with a friendly match contested between Parkhouse and Third Lanark at Beresford Park on New Year's Day 1900. A disappointing attendance was attributed to people being frightened away by the thought of being accosted by collection boxes. The pre-publicity had made a virtue of the fact that there would be a collection for the War Fund. Even with due allowance for inflation the £4 yielded by the box collection was, at best, moderate.

Two days earlier, on the last Saturday of the nineteenth century, Parkhouse had drawn 2-2 at Stranraer in a challenge match in aid of a local war relief fund. In relation to some smart marksmanship on the part of one of their inside-forwards it was written: "It is said that Billy Spence, after his experience at Stranraer, has volunteered for the Artillery in the Transvaal." This was a fleeting hint of media humour at a time when the locals were becoming conditioned to reading about the tyranny and corruption of Kruger and an intense Boer hostility to all things British.

The Billy Spence shooting analogy was most pertinent. On Friday, 5th January, 1900, the Ayrshire Yeomanry held tests at Kingcase for those civilians who had already passed the medical examination. The tests were for shooting and riding. One third were rejected on account of their shooting.

Notwithstanding the exacting standards of the Ayrshire Yeomanry, army recruitment continued unabated. For the last three months of 1899 recruitment in Ayr was up almost six-fold in comparison with the same period in 1898. Overcoming the bonds of home and family life would have been a consideration for many of them but few would have considered it a wrench to miss the action at Somerset or Beresford Parks. Ayr FC cobbled ingloriously to an eight-placed finish in a ten-club Second Division. Parkhouse had thus far not ascended to the hallowed sphere of the Scottish League and there was no discernible cup success for either club.

On the Saturday evening of 27th January, 1900, Parkhouse held a function in the Ayrshire and Galloway Hotel. It was in honour of one of their players, Trooper Joe Johnston, who had volunteered for active service in South Africa. The dearth of such functions was testimony to a reluctance of patriotism on the part of his team mates and Ayr FC counterparts.

On completion of the Second Division campaign, Ayr FC set about the task of completing their fixtures in the Scottish County League. Their opponents were East Stirling, Motherwell, Raith Rovers, Hamilton Accies and Abercorn. By the third week in April the obvious apathy drove an *Ayrshire Post* journalist to recommend the advisability of the local clubs bringing the season to a premature end. Ayr FC had just beaten Raith Rovers 3-1 in the Scottish County League and, across town, Parkhouse had beaten Dumfries 4-3 in a friendly. This did not appease the scribe who wrote in candid terms.

"For all that the Ayr public seem to care, the Ayr and Parkhouse Football Clubs might shut up their concerns for the season. At both Somerset and Beresford Parks on Saturday the spectators were only a few hundred strong. Ayr would certainly drop a considerable amount of money, and if Dumfries had at all a respectable guarantee the Parkhouse must also have been out of pocket. It is all bad enough with the teams clashing their fixtures, but when the latter happens attendances are pitiably small. What is it that ails the public I do not profess to know, but certain it is that they are taking little or no interest in the two Auld Toon football teams' performances. Matters will get worse if the relations between the clubs continue to be as strained as they are. Of course, my idea is that there should not be two clubs at all, but only one good one – with a solid town's support. As matters stand at present, we'll never have a good team in Ayr."

The amalgamation argument was a potent one albeit that it was not original. As early as the summer of 1893 talk had circulated about the wisdom of a united club in the town. The non-materialisation of the idea could, to a substantial extent, be explained by the reference to the strained relations mentioned in the piece just quoted. A state of simmering resentment existed. Parkhouse arranging the Dumfries friendly on the date of a scheduled match at Somerset Park could easily have been defined as a typically mean action.

In contrast the conduct of the war always stood to unite local opinion. For example news of the relief of Mafeking brought scenes of mass hysteria to the town whilst similar rejoicing was replicated the length and breadth of Britain. Mafeking was a British-occupied town under siege from Boer forces. Under the command of Robert Baden-Powell the siege was repelled for seven months from October 1899. When a British relief column arrived to fight off the Boer menace and bring relief to Mafeking, the celebrations at home might have given rise to an impression that the war had been won. The news reached Ayr late on the Friday night of 18th May, 1900.

"The news came when the town was getting ready to go to bed, when the shops were all shut and when the burghers were in carpet shoes and by the fireside. Upon ears that were not anticipating the noise of elation there fell the sound of distant cheering, then of hurrying feet, then of the bells ringing out into the clear May night, then of a louder cheering and more yelling and hurrying; and many a douce citizen called anew for his boots and rushed forth to join the throng to whom the glad tidings was common property. There are times when it seems as if a community was electrified and when the current of sympathy affects them all in similar fashion, just as there are occasions that from their very nature make Jack as good as his master, one man as good as another. And Friday night was one of these. The Ayr bells were never designed to ring merry peels. But the spirit to rejoice was there on Friday night and the solemnest clang of the big bell sounded joy upon the summer air."

Therein we have a telling piece of social commentary. Jack was as good as his master on this occasion but, by implication, pitched up short at other times. It was a phase of history when class divisions were most pronounced. Social attitudes even pervaded the hostility between Ayr FC and Parkhouse. Then, as now, the southern part of the town was more prosperous. Somerset Park, by reason of its proximity, drew support from the working class districts of Newton and Wallacetown. Beresford Park drew on support from the affluent areas on the other side of the river. Parkhouse did not renounce amateurism until 20th October, 1905 and even after that date the club held moral superiority over their northern brethren. The premise here is one of crowd disorder.

Moving on from this digression into social attitudes it may be told that the relief of Mafeking caused the streets of Ayr to be filled with cheering, hurrying throngs who laughed, shook hands and produced flags. Tree branches, grocers' boxes, cycle cases and packing paraphernalia got used for the purpose of kindling bonfires. Fireworks were let off and the fronts of houses quickly became decorated with bunting. The focal point was just outside Beresford Park but it has to be admitted that this was merely coincidental to the Burns Statue Square location. It was a scene of most macabre celebration.

"A crowd gathered by the burning grocery boxes under the shadow of the Burns Statue. The girls, barefooted, dishevelled, yelling, danced around the bonfire, waving branches of trees, reaching notes in the higher vocalisation never attempted by the foremost opera singers of the century, and evolving steps in dancing of a weirdness and originality sufficient to raise the hair on the head of a dancing master. Such music as there was to tear the spheres and to test such resisting capacity as there was in the drums of the ears of some fifteen hundred or two thousand of Her Majesty's loyal and devoted lieges, was supplied by about a dozen young men who played unheard of airs, but all extremely fitting to the occasion, on broken tea trays and empty biscuit boxes. An experience such as that of the Burns Statue Square is apt to shake one's pre-conceived ideas regarding the beating of gongs and the playing upon tom-toms, and to modify the rather jaundiced and prejudiced conception that the ordinary Briton has for the night harmonies of the male cat."

It all persisted until "the midnight moon had risen and even until the coming sun was throwing his beams upon the eastern horizon." On the Saturday the celebrations resumed.

I can recall being told by my grandmother about the celebrations in her home town of Haddington. The relief of Mafeking took place one month after her fourteenth birthday and her recollection was of a bonfire upon which an effigy of Kruger was burned.

It is beyond doubt that the burning of a Kruger effigy would have been a widespread practice throughout the land. Jingoism and propaganda remained unabated in its capacity to fuel the mood of the British public. To compare anyone with a Boer was tantamount to the supreme insult and that was what happened after Ayr FC played a third round Scottish Qualifying Cup tie at Galston on 6th November, 1900.

That a formidable tie was anticipated can be accredited to the fact that Galston were the holders of the Scottish Qualifying Cup. The ground name, Riverside Park, was understated. It looked as if the river had already joined the pitch. Large pools of water, several inches deep, lay on the playing surface. In some parts the touchline was submerged from view. The consensus was that the referee would order a postponement after a cursory glance. In the event his inexplicable verdict was – Game On! To compound the issue the rain continued to batter down and a badly deteriorated pitch deteriorated further thereby drawing a comparison with a swamp. "The splashing was equal to the attempts of juvenile bathers" opined one onlooker. "WATER POLO AT RIVERSIDE PARK" stated a headline. The Ayr support exceeded 200 and they were in good cheer as they watched a 4-2 win. However their happy demeanour aroused ire in the locals. Throughout the tie fighting took place around the ropes. It continued in the streets after the match. The scale of intimidation induced the *Ayrshire Post* football writer to fear for his safety, even going so far as to express the relief he felt when reaching the safety of a carriage in a train at Galston Station. Ensconced in the safe environs of his Nile Court office, he was able to fearlessly document this view: "For swearing the Galston crowd are most certainly due the Oculeus cookie with the glossy skin." Translating this into modern day terminology it can be interpreted that they took the biscuit! It was a tame rebuke. The *Ayr Observer* reporter had no inhibitions when offering the most damning criticism the Galston support could have been subjected to: "In the knowledge that they were present in overwhelming odds they did what otherwise would have been craven cowardice in the knowledge that there was safety in numbers, and instituted a series of bullying tactics discreditable to the worst type of Boer."

The course of the war was understandably conducive to the local and national mood. The relief of Mafeking was instrumental in massively raising the country's morale much in the way that the relief of Kimberley and the relief of Ladysmith had done at earlier dates. Human emotion was, is, and forever will be fickle. The elation receded when the conflict and the consequent casualty rate escalated. From the description of frenetical surreality in Burns Statue Square in May 1900 the depths of despair were described in similarly emotive tones in December when the *Ayrshire Post* observed that: "The year that is closing is beyond any doubt whatever, so far as this country is concerned, the most unsatisfactory year, the most deplorable year, in every way the year that can least stand scrutiny, within the memory of this generation. It has been a year of war, cursed with bloodshed. It has been a year of administrative bungling. It has been a year of the piling up of debt." The list of misery went on and on but this is enough to clarify the gist.

On 19th January, 1901, Ayr FC had a first round Scottish Cup replay away to the Aberdeen-based Orion. On the Friday the *Ayrshire Post* readers were informed that: "The Ayr team will entrain for the seat of war at 3.45 p.m. today." Transcending from the metaphorical to the actual, the Ayrshire Yeomanry did entrain for the seat of war from the same location. This fact was recalled for the purpose of drawing a comparison with the departure of the supporters on the morning of the match. Punctuating football coverage in this way was a clear indication that the war remained close to the public conscience. That conscience was on the verge of being jarred.

On the day that Ayr FC played and won their tie at Aberdeen, the newspapers contained the first intimation that Queen Victoria was seriously ill. On Tuesday, 22nd January, she passed away at 6.45 p.m. It was the termination of a reign dating back to 1837.

On Saturday 26th January, St. Mirren came to Ayr for a second round Scottish Cup tie. It was a brief reprieve pending postponements on the following Saturday, the day of the state funeral. Both teams wore mourning armlets out of respect for the late Queen. Wintry showers of sleet and rain conspired with a 3-1 defeat to further suppress local cheer. John McDonald (future Blackburn Rovers) sliced an own goal past his brother Hugh (future Woolwich Arsenal) in the Ayr goal. This calamity was blamed on "the vagaries of the wind." The crowd was estimated at 2,000 and a goodly number of them would have been suffering far greater vagaries through the privations of home life. Those privations were expressed loudly and eloquently from a pulpit.

The Rev. Millar Patrick was not the type of person one would wish to have for company on a night out. At the Trinity United Free Church in Ayr he delivered fire and brimstone sermons that were guaranteed to keep his congregation in a highly attentive state. On the evening of 3rd March, 1901, he was at his fiery best.

"The conscience of the people has been too long lulled and dragged and the fact is that there is much crime and misery and sin that are cursing the town, for which God will charge the bill to us."

The Rev. Patrick's contemporaries viewed him as a religious zealot. Perhaps he was, but he cared deeply about local poverty and deprivation. His sermon that night was not confined to thundering rhetoric. It contained information culled from the burgh medical officer's report and a lecture delivered by the county Procurator Fiscal. In forcible terms he appraised the congregation of the following facts.

- Mortality across the river (Newton and Wallacetown) is much greater than on the southern side.
- Dwellings are unhealthy and insanitary on the northern side.
- Ayr stands third among Scottish towns, next to Glasgow and Greenock in evil repute for criminality.
- For drunkenness it has the unhappy distinction of standing first among Scottish towns.

Ayr Town Council convened a special meeting to talk about the housing issue. Picking through a report by the Public Health Committee was an alarming exercise.

- Lasy year over 200 houses in Ayr were inhabited though condemned by the sanitary authorities as unfit for human habitation.
- The infant mortality is enormous. It is greater in Ayr than in Glasgow.
- The average duration of life on the north side of the river is under thirty years.
- There are hundreds of citizens, whatever their desire, who have absolutely no alternative but to live in uninhabitable houses.

To put it into context, the crowds at Somerset Park were principally drawn from a locality with an average life expectancy of less than thirty years and second only to Glasgow and Greenock for crime whilst topping the table for convictions for drunkenness. So did the council do anything to alleviate the plight of the people? Yes, on 7th August, on the motion of Captain Galloway, it was agreed that juvenile offenders would be whipped!

From the mortality statistics it should not be deduced that people in these districts were unlikely to live beyond the age of thirty. The high rate of child mortality impacted adversely on the overall average. Taking the town as a whole, there were 656 deaths recorded in 1901. Seventy-three were between the ages of seventy and eighty, twenty-eight were between eighty and ninety and three were over ninety, the highest age being ninety-three. From that we know that 552 out of 656 did not attain the age of seventy. That is disheartening when the superior survival rate south of the river is factored in.

From the Victorian period through to the Edwardian era and beyond there is ample evidence of bad behaviour at Somerset Park. While not looking to excuse it, at least there were socio-economic factors to explain it.

Such living conditions might also explain the seeming lust for adventure imbibed in so many of the army recruits. A smart uniform, regular food, hero status and foreign travel – it is an inescapable conclusion that some were incentivised by thinking that anything had to be better than their current mode of life. The risk was the potential for a gory death. Craigmillar Buildings, in King Street, had a Boer War legacy. It became known as the Spion Kop. This was the name of a Boer-held hill considered to be of strategic importance to the British. Between 23rd and 24th January, 1900, a battle ensued to seize control of the hill. It was a failed battle resulting in slaughter and it went down in history as one of Britain's great military blunders. Quite why this scene of misery became synonymous with a block of flats in Ayr can only be guessed at although it does allude to unpleasantness.

The point that Parkhouse populated a more prosperous part of the town and attracted a well-heeled support has already been identified as a factor in the rivalry between the clubs. Perhaps this explanation of the extent of the gulf in wealth will permit an understanding of the intensity and scale of the bitterness that openly existed. In the present day the fiercest club rivalry in the world is arguably that between the Argentinian clubs Boca Juniors and River Plate. The resentment is based on the same principle as existed all those years ago for Ayr FC and Parkhouse. Boca Juniors has traditionally been the club for the working man. As for River Plate you only require to know their nickname ... Los Millonarios.

At the conclusion of season 1900/01 it was evident that attending Somerset Park had been a positive form of escapism from the domestic squalor. Ayr FC succeeded in winning every home match in the Second Division campaign. In contrast every away league match was lost. Crossing the Pow Burn seemed to have a negative effect on the team's form ... but only in the league. In an Ayrshire Cup final replay Stevenston Thistle, nicknamed the Dynamitards, were beaten at Kilmarnock's Rugby Park. It was a major achievement, no Ayr club having won the competition since its inception in season 1877/78. The club secretary wrote to Doctor Naismith, who had a long association with Ayr FC and was also a member of Ayr Cricket Club. In the capacity of senior medical officer with Pilcher's Column, he was engaged in harrowing work at the seat of war. From his heartfelt reply it was gratifying to know that the Ayrshire Cup win had raised his spirits. Addressed from Brandfort Camp he wrote:

"I regret I have not been very able to answer your last letter to me as we have for months past been trekking and fighting daily. I may say that for a whole year we have not been halted for seven days anywhere and no column in South Africa has done harder or more harassing work. I seldom see our casualties reported and as there is no war correspondent with us, for which in some ways we have reason to be thankful, I hardly ever see any account of our fighting in the home papers. We get the Ayr papers out here so I am fairly well up in all the Auld Toon news. Thank you for your letter. I am delighted to hear of the success of the old club in the matter of the cup after so many years hard work. Kindly convey to the committee my hearty and sincere congratulations and also my acceptance with many thanks for the honour they have again conferred on me, of the presidency of the club. I was unable to convey your information to the Royal Scots Fusiliers for we have no idea where they are and never get any news. Like ourselves, however, they no doubt see the local papers."

Sent from Brandfort Camp! Oh dear! The connotations are dark, very dark. By this stage of the war the Boers were conducting guerrilla warfare. To counteract this the British decided to clear large areas of the countryside and concentrate the civilian population into camps. These were the twentieth century's first concentration camps. There was no deliberate policy to starve these people but the scale of numbers rendered it beyond anyone's capacity to adequately feed them all. Moreover inadequate sanitation allowed disease to spread quickly. The number of women and children who died at Brandfort Concentration Camp during the Boer conflict amounted to 15,550. When the British press referred to concentration camps this was not done in a metaphorical context. The horror was on a scale too large to suppress but when people in Britain complained they were labelled pro-Boer.

On 26th September, 1901, Ayr's electric trams ran for the first time. This mode of transport had the promise of allowing easier access to the town's football grounds for the populace for whom distance was a factor. Significantly the inaugural date was a Thursday. A vigorous campaign of dissent had been simmering from people who felt aggrieved by the intention to run the trams on Sundays. It was an issue that had the Rev. Millar Patrick at his vocal best. He spoke fervently about the threat of secularisation of the Sabbath. His protestations were to no avail. A counter argument was that the trams assisted people to get to church. Regardless of the merits and demerits of trams on a Sunday, any disturbance must have been minimal. They were not reputed for speed. It was passed on for posterity that people would opt to journey on foot if time was too pressing. In evidence it may be considered that, in March 1902, Glasgow Corporation got fined £10 in each of two charges brought against them by a private citizen, of running trams at a speed exceeding eight miles an hour.

On 15th December, 1901, the Rev. Patrick again preached with his customary fury. He denounced those who attended football matches at Beresford Park and Somerset Park, claiming that the fierce excitement unfitted them for the spiritual interests of life. In the same sermon theatre-goers also bore the brunt of his disfavour when he declared that he considered himself to be personally barred from entering a theatre. Attending a theatre show was a bawdy experience in this phase of history but people needed a diversion from the news of the war in South Africa and, perhaps more pertinently, a diversion from their living conditions. Even with the considerable benefit of hindsight it has to be conceded that watching matches at Somerset Park was apt to be less than serene but his judgement of attendees at Beresford Park was open to question. Running parallel to Beresford Terrace, that ground was just a short distance from his own church, located in Midton Road. The church is still there, albeit that it is no longer known as the Trinity United Free. Today it is known as St. Columba's. When the legendary Ayr United manager Ally MacLeod passed away, his funeral service was conducted there. Footballing greats who attended included Manchester United boss Alex Ferguson. It is a great irony that a football-themed funeral was held in a church from which a former minister had been passionate in his denunciation of the game. On 6th February, 2004, the Rev. Fraser Aitken spoke sincerely about Ally MacLeod's role as a family man. His address came from the same pulpit used by the Rev. Millar Patrick when he was thundering disapproval of local issues. In his defence it may be observed that Patrick was a man of strong principle.

There is a further irony. Football in Ayr evolved in his own parish. His church lay in clear sight of the Springvale Park ground. The site of other pioneering grounds lay in reasonable proximity; Ballantine Drive, Robbsland Park (off St.Leonard's Road) and the Racecourse (old). He was not totally devoid of sporting interest and could be spotted regularly at Dam Park, cricket being within the bounds of his standards of morality. Taking into account his views on the sanctity of the Sabbath and his antipathy towards football we know that his opinion of Sunday football would have sent his fury into overdrive. Not until 10th February, 1974, did a senior football match take place in Ayr on a Sunday (Ayr United 3 Dunfermline Athletic 1). Those of us who were in the 6,589 crowd can be most grateful that we will not be accountable to the Rev. Patrick on judgement day!

"The year 1901 – the first of the new century – has left an unenviable mark upon the history, not only of Great Britain, but also of the whole world, which will ever make it a notable date to all time, seeing that at the commencement the good and great Queen Victoria ended her long and glorious reign."

The local newspaper summarising 1901 in this way also carried a piece about the progress of the war being slow under Lord Kitchener. For writers of this time the default mode when discussing Queen Victoria was one of fawning praise. The inhabitants of the hovels of Newton and Wallacetown, had they been canvassed for an opinion, may have been more restrained on the viewpoint that Victoria's reign was glorious. Theirs was an existence bereft of glory.

Commando raids are a common tactic of war and there are numerous tales of such deployments in the Boer War. But a commando raid undertaken by civilians has to be considered a rarity and this tale is spiced by the involvement of a one-time Ayr footballer.

The first senior football club in Ayr was Ayr Thistle, founded in 1872 by a group of lads who used to meet on the steps at the foot of Wellington Lane. Their earliest matches were played on the Low Green. In 1876/77, by which time their home was Robbsland Park, they had a magnificent Scottish Cup run. When Ayr United reached the semi-finals of the Scottish Cup in 1973 it was popularly misconceived that this was the first Ayr team to reach that stage of the competition. In fact Ayr Thistle had played in a Scottish Cup semi-final on 13th January, 1877. Opposed by Vale of Leven at Kinning Park, the ground of Rangers, their chances of victory were non-existent. In their quarter-final played on 30th December, 1876, Vale of Leven had beaten the best team in the world, Queen's Park. Founded in 1867, this was the first defeat in their history. Earlier in 1876 Queen's Park had conceded their first ever goal, also against Vale of Leven. Nine years without conceding a goal! Vale of Leven, in line with expectation, easily progressed to the 1877 Scottish Cup final. They beat Ayr Thistle 9-0. Captain of the Ayr Thistle team was Harry Fullarton, one of the six forwards in the then standard 2 : 2 : 6 formation.

Harry was well known locally. He excelled in athletics and his father was Bailie Alexander Fullarton. Emigrating to

South Africa he settled at a farm called Waaikraal, an unsafe location during the Boer War. In January 1902 predictions of the end of the war began to gather currency. The belief, whether substantiated or not, was that the Boer defence was broken. Ordinary mortals in Harry Fullarton's situation would have been happy to sit out the war at this stage. He was not an ordinary mortal. At a farm two miles away lived Mark Killan, a colonial rebel. The expression *colonial rebel* is not wholly explicit although it does concede enough to clarify that it was someone detrimental to the British cause. That was the interpretation of Harry. Together with his son, also called Harry, and a Mr Heberden, a sortie was made for the purpose of capturing Killan. Captaining Ayr Thistle to victory over Vale of Leven in a Scottish Cup semi-final carried the hallmark of a mission destined for certain failure but here in early 1902 his life, that of his son and of a colleague were at risk if the venture failed. It is unlikely that a Boer sympathiser in a war-torn region could have been spoken into coming quietly. The mission succeeded. Killan was handed over to the Willowmore District Mounted Troops. The British General commanding the district did not deem this to be civilian interference. He made special mention of it in a report.

Twenty-five fatalities in a time of war is not a large amount in overall scale - not that this should be read as a slur against those who have fought bravely for their country. On 5th April, 1902, that number of fatalities occurred about six thousand miles from the South African war – at Ibrox Park. Ten minutes into a Scotland versus England game a section of terracing collapsed when the supporting wooden joists gave way. Andy Aitken, then of Newcastle United and formerly of Parkhouse, was a native of Ayr who was in the Scotland team on that day. Other Ayrshire players in the team were Alec Brown from Glenbuck, Bobby Templeton from Coylton and Nick Smith from Darvel. Peter McBride, originally a goalkeeper for Ayr FC and then of Preston North End, attended the match with his arm in a sling and had the illusion of being one of the casualties. In an act of dubious stoicism the disaster did not lead to an abandonment. It merely deferred proceedings for twenty-one minutes and a 1-1 draw was played out.

On 17th May, Ayr FC and Kilmarnock played in a 1-1 draw at Somerset Park. It was a match staged in aid of the Ibrox Disaster Fund, £39:14s being raised. With peace talks being under way, it would have been futile to give any consideration to a similar charity match for war funds.

The Boer surrender was concluded on 31st May, a Saturday. To the population of Ayr the signing of the peace treaty remained an unknown fact beyond that date. At about 10 p.m. on the Sunday night the news reached the town in a telephone call to Provost Thomas Templeton at his home in Monument Road. The magnitude of a vicious war being at an end appeared to be lost on him. He kept the news to himself! An *Ayrshire Post* scribe couched it in more diplomatic terms.

"Provost Templeton, on receipt of the information, considering the lateness of the hour, deemed it inexpedient to take any steps in the direction of conveying the intelligence to the community."

On the Monday his inexpediency gathered momentum when he departed for Glasgow on council business and left it to the townsfolk to read the news in the morning papers.

However, this hint of criticism can be spectacularly redressed by his various roles in developing football in the town. He was a founding member of Ayr Thistle when they began playing on the Low Green in 1872. Then when Ayr Thistle amalgamated with Ayr Academicals to form Ayr FC in 1879 he became a supporter of that club. He then followed Parkhouse whilst they made the transition from juniors into seniors and he had a spell as president. In 1910 he was a neutral participant in the amalgamation talks between Parkhouse and Ayr FC prior to becoming a regular supporter of the newly-formed Ayr United right up until an illness preceded his death at the age of sixty-three in August 1918.

The people were not so inhibited as their Provost. Word spread rapidly. There had been joy in the town on 22nd March, 1902, when Parkhouse returned home from Kilmarnock having beaten Galston for custody of the Ayrshire Cup. Perhaps this should be qualified by stating that there had been joy in part of the town. Now we had an event guaranteed to unite the social divide.

Between noon and one o'clock the bells rung out on the steeple and the Wallace Tower. There was no official recognition. It will be recalled that the Provost was in Glasgow and so too were the Dean of Guild and the Town Clerk.

Flags, bunting and streamers were displayed and not just on buildings. The trams too were bedecked. Children in the elementary schools were sent home and some of the works observed the day as a holiday. In the evening the burgh band boarded a tram and played patriotic music while cyclists followed keeping time to the music with their bells. Mobbed streets and processions indicated extreme merriment. In the circumstances it was all well behaved and there was scarcely any need for intervention by the police . . . until about eleven o'clock! From then on there was a lot of rowdyism. It was on a scale high enough to prompt a headline of HOOLIGANISM RAMPANT. In the ensuing havoc Beresford Park fell victim. The chief manifestation of the disorder was the creation of bonfires in the streets. That in itself was acceptable but some of the blazes prompted police intervention through being perilously close to buildings. One bonfire was kindled close enough to the Clydesdale Bank as to cause a window to crack in the intense heat. An anxiety to procure anything flammable was another issue for the patrolling constables. As long as it burned few were too discerning about the consequences of dismantling fences or stealing other property. Two constables were assaulted when trying to prevent more items being put onto a bonfire situated just a few yards from a shop at the Fish Cross. Further up the town they did not have the convenience of fish boxes and fish barrels for fuel. In an attempt to requisition firewood a portion of the Beresford Park stand was destroyed. The dual motive of a dislike of Parkhouse would be a neat theory but there is no evidence to support it.

Retrieval of the bunting was necessary that summer. The coronation of King Edward VII took place on 9th August, 1902. His death on 6th May, 1910, signalled the end of the Edwardian era; by then it was the threshold of the most important date in Ayr United's history. 9th May, 1910, was the date of the meeting that ratified the amalgamation between Ayr FC and Parkhouse to form the club. The closeness of these dates meant that the birth of Ayr United was reported in newspapers with black borders on the pages.

That the town of Ayr was skilled at celebrating was consistent with the frequency with which it was practised. A year containing the Boer surrender and the coronation further contained the seventh centenary of Ayr becoming a Royal Burgh. In 1952 Ayr United beat Queen's Park in a one-off revival of the Ayr Charity Cup brought about by the 750th anniversary of the Royal Burgh. In 2005 Hibs were beaten at Ayr in a shootout after a drawn match in the Ayr Guildry Cup, a trophy put up in commemoration of the eighth centenary of the town's Royal Burgh status. Let us recap. 700th anniversary in 1902, 750th anniversary in 1952 and 800th anniversary in 2005. The figures do not add up and here is why. By 2005 it had been established beyond doubt that the royal charter was signed in 1205 and not in 1202.

2

The Great War

On the Tuesday night of 4th August, 1914, the Foreign Office issued this statement.

"Owing to the summary rejection by the German Government of the request made by His Majesty's Government for assurances that the neutrality of Belgium will be respected, His Majesty's Ambassador to Berlin has received his passports, and His Majesty's Government declared to the German Government that a state of war exists between Great Britain and Germany as from 11 p.m. on 4th August."

Those terse and formal words propelled the country towards a conflict that would see death and carnage on an industrial scale. Why was this happening? As the statement makes plain the neutrality of Belgium had not been respected. Yet surely there had to be more to it. Yes, there was more to it although not much. Entire books have been written about the origin of this conflict but it can be summarised in concise terms. A Serbian called Gavrilo Princip assassinated Franz Ferdinand in Sarajevo on 28th June, 1914. Austria, in its determination to assert authority over Serbia, opportunistically issued an ultimatum. Acceptance by Serbia would have meant an erosion of its independence. The consequent non-acceptance gave Austria an excuse to declare war on Serbia. Russia took the side of Serbia thereby putting themselves at war with Austria. Germany considered itself to be an ally of Austria and, on that basis, declared war on Russia. France, an ally of Russia, refused a German demand to stay neutral. That put

This image was taken right outside Somerset Park. It is from a postcard sent on 4th February, 1914.

The view in February 2014.

Germany at war with France. Germany attacked France by the shortest route. That route was through Belgium. This was in breach of an old treaty of which Britain was a signatory. It stated that Belgium's neutrality would not be violated. Hence local tensions in the Balkans (local in global terms) created a war involving all those major powers. Eminent historians such as A. J. P. Taylor have articulated it all in forensic scrutiny. For this book a 'Higher History at Ayr Academy'-style summary should suffice!

As with the outbreak of the Boer War we have the mandatory ultimatum and the mandatory grievance. This time the mandatory villain was Kaiser Wilhelm, the German Emperor. And the mandatory "all over by Christmas" prophecies? Yes, but it was not a consensus. Trawling through newspapers of the time indicates that there were commentators bracing themselves for a long war.

There were still people living in Ayr who could recall the Crimean War (1853-1856) and, of course, the Boer War remained vivid in the memory. These were not isolated conflicts. The Zulu War of 1879 and the First Boer War (1880-1881) were just two others in the list of wars engaged in during the intermediate period. This declaration in 1914 created palpable nervousness amongst the German residents in Ayr and district. Two of them who had been staying in the town for more than two decades applied for British Citizenship in a fit of panic. It cost them £10 each. Others headed in haste for their native country. It was the correct course of action. On the Wednesday evening of 23rd September five Germans resident in the town were arrested and taken under police escort to Edinburgh's Redford Barracks where they were detained as prisoners of war. It was a nationwide practice to detain males who were of an eligible age for military service. In consequence twenty-six Germans had their names on the registration books kept by the Chief Constable of the Burgh. Three Germans in Ayr who were eligible for detention did manage to evade capture but they were arrested in the town four weeks later.

Johnny Crosbie - The club agreed to pay him half wages while on military service.

On the Wednesday evening of 5th August the regular reserves of the Royal Scots Fusiliers marched from the barracks located on the present day site of The Citadel. The hundreds of people gathered outside the barracks followed them on their way as they proceeded by way of Fort Street and Miller Road to Ayr Station. En route the pipes and drums from the depot played military music as they marched along to loud cheering from the crowds on the pavements. On arrival at Burns Statue Square the mass of humanity could be numbered in thousands. The detachment then experienced problems in negotiating through the station entrance so dense was the crowd.

"The emotions could not help being stirred at the sight of those poor fellows, leaving wives and weans, mothers and sisters behind them, and going off to – God alone knows what. A determined set of men, hard and tough with toil, and seemingly in fighting condition. I am sure that everyone who watched the departure of these detachments of the Royal Scots Fusiliers from Ayr, in their hearts were praying for victory to their arms and a safe return, when they may count on a great welcome."

They departed for Gosport on the south coast since that was where the regiment was stationed. Poignant indeed though is the above reference to them departing to "God alone knows what."

On the day of their departure and on the following day, the local pubs were shut between 3 p.m. and 7 p.m. in compliance with a request from the military authorities. Ayr Races, after communication with the Jockey Club, were abandoned for the next Friday and Saturday 14th and 15th August. Ayr United were due to host Partick Thistle in the season's inaugural First Division fixture on Saturday 15th. The likelihood of it going ahead was rendered vulnerable.

On the day the war began, but before it was actually underway, the mere inevitability of it created a wave of panic-stricken people laying siege to the local shops in order to horde food. Contemporaries were unequivocal in their condemnation of this practice and were quick to ridicule the notion that the country was facing starvation. Yet the march of time would prove that the notion was not entirely ridiculous.

Pub opening hours restricted (albeit temporarily), Ayr Races abandoned and panic buying of food – this was the reality (or surreality!) before the war had properly warmed up. For Ayr United there could be no escaping the impact.

1st August was the last peace time Saturday. In heat described as "almost tropical in character" a practice match between teams of Ayr United players took place at Beresford Park. In front of a large crowd the recognised first team won 6-2 in a match in which Jimmy Richardson scored four. A second practice match was scheduled for the same venue on the next Saturday. However the immediate future of the Scottish game was quickly immersed in deep uncertainty.

Well-founded speculation arose that the Scottish Football League would be considering the question of postponing the opening of the league season. Mobilisation had been immediate and it was beyond doubt that the movement of other units would deprive clubs of a significant number of their players. Ayr United were not immune. Johnny Crosbie, Neil McBain and John Bellringer were already enlisted. Crosbie and McBain would become club legends. Bellringer's fate was to make the supreme sacrifice without becoming a club luminary. All three played in that first trial match. One week later, with the sides again styled 'A' team and 'B' team, they were all absent for reasons of military duty. The 'A' team won 6-0 and for the second half the half-back lines were swapped over. No one was imperilled by such manoeuvring, in contrast to the military planning of the generals on whom lay the aspirations and hopes of a nation. A low turnout for the follow-up practice match was not entrenched in the priorities of the people as much as the incessant rainfall.

An historic decision was made by the Ayr United board. The club colours of crimson and gold were being ditched in favour of black and white hooped shirts and black shorts. Would it be a new dawn or would the club be facing the metaphorical dusk of football being abandoned altogether?

The league season did succeed in getting underway though this was tempered by extreme dubiety about its continuance. In thrashing Partick Thistle 4-0 at Somerset Park there was a return of the "almost tropical heat". Johnny Crosbie was a conspicuous absentee; in an outstanding gesture by the Ayr United directors, it was agreed to pay him half wages while on military service. As a native of Glenbuck he lived close to the Ayrshire-Lanarkshire border. He could just as easily have been with the Ayrshire Yeomanry as the Lanarkshire Yeomanry. As a Territorial he was called up by the Lanarkshire Yeomanry.

Graphic accounts of German atrocities in Belgium began to appear in the local newspapers. There is a strong probability that these were Press Association reports. In anticipation that these reports would be dismissed as propaganda it was stated:

"The accounts from which we have quoted were prepared by the highest judicial and university authorities of Belgium and it cannot be suggested that they are faked."

It being enlistment rather than conscription at this stage, the Government and military authorities had to strive hard to appeal to the sensibilities of potential recruits. If believed, the revulsion reported from Belgium would have been a potent incentive. Not until 1916 did military service become compulsory. With each passing day the morality of football's continuance was growing ever more contentious. Arguments of justification were minimal. A welcome diversion from the anxiety of war was one defence. The opportunity to raise funds by collecting from the crowds was another. Pro-football lobbying began and ended on these two points.

The second home league match of the season brought Airdrie to Somerset Park for a scoreless draw. A crowd figure exceeding 5,000 gave credence to the view that a goodly number of the public did see it as a means of diverting attention from the fighting. Part two of the argument was borne out by Red Cross nurses turning up with collection boxes.

On Tuesday, 8th September, 1914, Ayr United director Tom Steen presided over a meeting of the Emergency and Finance Committee of the Scottish Football Association. A deputation had already visited London and their report was submitted for discussion at this meeting. The deputation had been received at the War Office. Inescapable is the view that the personnel in that department would have had more urgent priorities than discussing Scottish football. Nevertheless it was all constructive and the delegates left with the unanimous opinion that the Scottish game should not be suspended. The justification was almost predictable. Clubs under S.F.A. jurisdiction would be able to render valuable assistance in matters of recruitment and raising money for relief purposes. Relief? Wasn't this the terminology of charitable giving in the Boer War? Yes, and it gave more than a hint that women would be widowed and potentially left destitute. It was a practical line of thinking and not in the least far-fetched.

The S.F.A. was most fortunate in having someone of Tom Steen's calibre presiding over a meeting on this scale of importance. He was skilled in the art of persuasion and a thorough organiser. In 1903 his power of oratory was perhaps the only factor in gaining entry to the Second Division for his club Parkhouse. Had merit been the guiding factor Parkhouse's case would not have stood scrutiny. In 1913 his negotiation skills were also influential in gaining Ayr United's admission to the First Division notwithstanding the absurdity of the need to negotiate. The absurdity alludes to the fact that Ayr United had just retained the Second Division championship. Steen, whose family owned the Ayrshire and Galloway Hotel, was small in build and large in stature. It is a common trait to talk for the sake of talking but when Steen did the talking you could be sure that it would be backed-up by meaningful action. So it was agreed that the member clubs would be sent a list of proposals. The covering letter, signed by John McDowall, secretary, stated:

"I send you herewith copies of the proposals which have the approval of the War Office. I also send you a poster to be exhibited on football grounds. I shall be happy to send you as many copies as you require. Your club is earnestly asked to render every assistance and encouragement to secure recruits for the Army in the present great national emergency. To give effect to the proposals it is necessary that you should communicate with the recruiting officer for your district and arrange with him the best means to adopt for enrolling the recruits, either in your offices, or the nearest Army recruiting depot. Means should, if possible, be at hand for completing the enlistment."

The main proposals were:
- Clubs should place their grounds at the disposal of the War Office on days other than match days, for use as drill grounds, or as the service may require.
- Where football matches are played, arrangements are to be made for well-known public men to address the players and spectators, urging men who are physically fit, and otherwise able, to at once enlist.
- Where practicable recruiting stations are to be at or adjacent to grounds.
- Posters should be put up at the ground and in the programme of the club.
- It is hoped that where special matches are arranged, the whole of the net gate receipts will be given to a war relief fund.

The design and layout of the poster did not shirk from the gravity of Britain's situation.

Army recruitment drive at the Ayr United versus Morton match on 14th November, 1914.

THE WAR AND FOOTBALL
RECRUITS URGENTLY NEEDED FOR THE ARMY

The Scottish Football Association earnestly appeals to the patriotism of all who are interested in the game to support the nation in the present serious emergency, and, to those who are able to do so, to render personal service in the Army or the Royal Navy, which are so gallantly upholding our national honour.

RECRUITS FOR THE ARMY ARE AT THE MOMENT MOST URGENTLY NEEDED

Players and spectators who are physically fit, and otherwise able, are urged to

JOIN THE ARMY AT ONCE

The premise was straightforward. In Scotland the game would continue with the blessing of the War Office in return for co-operation with the war effort. No! That was the interpretation of the S.F.A. delegation but a War Office denial was issued. The official minute of the delegation read: "Having consulted the authorities the deputation is unanimously of the opinion that the playing of football in Scotland should not be suspended." In a conflicting statement Mr H.J. Tennant, Under-Secretary for War, said: "No objection is taken by the military authorities to occasional recreation. It is considered, however, that professional football does not come within that category, and that it can only be admitted on grounds of contract or employment. It is much more desirable that professional football players should find employment in His Majesty's Forces than in their old occupation. With regard to the question of breach of contract it is considered that this is a time when all should be prepared to make sacrifices."

So the quandary was this. The S.F.A.'s take on it was that continuance was alright in accordance with the consent of the War Office whilst the War Office remained unequivocal that there was a misinterpretation, therefore there was no consent. With breathtaking contempt the S.F.A. solved the issue very simply. At a meeting on 17th November, 1914, Morton's Duncan Campbell, presiding, said that he had been asked to say that "the statements which were made to the deputation which went to London to interview the War Office authorities were neither misunderstood nor misrepresented." On the basis of this disdain towards the War Office the case for abandoning the Scottish game was dismissed. There was a glimmer of a concession in the decision to suspend the Scottish Cup competition.

As with the Boer War the appeal to join up was extended far beyond our shores. Davie Hill was one of the Scotsmen who answered the call from Canada. Hill was a former left-back with Parkhouse. He played in their Ayrshire Cup winning team of 1902 and his last season at the club was 1904/05. That he then moved to Third Lanark was ample proof of his stature. Scottish champions 1903/04; Scottish Cup winners in 1904/05 – this was the level set by Third Lanark. Hill gained his one and only Scotland cap in 1906, it being the occasion of a 1-0 win in Dublin. Fittingly it was on St. Patrick's Day. Six weeks later he had another major match. It was the Scottish Cup final against Hearts. The cup was not retained and it went east after a 1-0 scoreline. Hill captained Third Lanark to a 4-0 victory over Celtic in the Glasgow Cup final of 1908/09. He sought his future across the Atlantic and by September 1914 it was reported that he was on his way to the front with the Canadian Engineering Corps. He survived the war, ultimately dying in May 1928 at a military hospital in Canada at the age of forty-six.

On the first Saturday of September Ayr United won 2-1 at Boghead Park, Dumbarton. Ladies collected for one of the war funds and recruiting officers mingled with spectators. On the same afternoon Ayr United reserves drew 0-0 with Clyde reserves in a Scottish 2nd XI Cup tie at Beresford Park. The Red Cross nurses, as at Somerset Park a week earlier, were in attendance with their collection boxes. It was unremitting. The pressure to donate to a variation of war charities was as unremitting as the pressure to enlist. Whether home or away, first team or reserve fixture, there was no respite. A visit to the High Street brought the likelihood of being confronted with a Flag Day. Neither was there immunity in workplaces.

With the Western Race Meeting being cancelled, the appetite for football was all the more insatiable. A special train was laid on for Ayr United's league trip to Kilmarnock. It was overcrowded ten minutes before the 2 p.m. departure and for that reason it did not stop at Newton, Prestwick or Troon. The scheduled service departed at 2.10 p.m. and picked up those left behind whilst cars, motorcycles and cycles converged on Rugby Park. In his passionate summary of Ayr's 2-1 win one scribe wrote: "We don't think anybody would presume to deny that the better team won, though the feeling of some Killie enthusiasts towards the United is somewhat akin to that of Germany towards Britain."

Khaki was in evidence all round the ground when Ayr United went to Easter Road to play Hibs. A large contingent of the wearers of the khaki were members of the Ayrshire Yeomanry, stationed at Cupar. Their leave for the day was well spent watching Jimmy Richardson scoring a hat-trick in a 4-0 win. Once more there was an emotive analogy.

"If General French's British troops, with their French allies, come out as successfully in their left wing work as Gray and Cassidy did in theirs on Saturday, the Germans opposed to them will have some running (away) to do."

A week's leave of absence allowed Johnny Crosbie to be present at a home match with Celtic. An illness had laid him up in Glasgow's Stobhill Hospital so he was only able to spectate. Joe Cassidy scored the only goal of the match in the 73rd minute. Yes, the same Joe Cassidy who was on loan

Alec Gray scoring in a 2-1 win over Aberdeen on 18th April, 1914. It was the club's last home league fixture prior to the outbreak of war.

to Ayr United from Celtic. In the second half goalkeeper Jack Lyall had to leave the field after suffering a kick on the head from Patsy Gallagher. Jimmy Richardson deputised in goal but had nothing to do and the Ayr goal even came during this phase. When Lyall reappeared with a bandaged head he looked like a casualty of war. In the ensuing years wounded Tommies were to become a common sight at home games.

"It is not often that on successive Saturdays two such prominent teams as Celtic and Rangers have the same journey to make and the same team to face; but that has occurred in Ayr United's fixtures with the two aforementioned Glasgow combinations. The story is an old one of the Celtic visit; they came they saw and fell. On Saturday last it was the Rangers' turn to lay siege to the Ayr United forces in their stronghold at Somerset Park and, as the old country woman said in regard to the news of the battle in the Boer War about which latter she had known nothing, they got a fine day for it."

A fine day for it! How apt. Beating Celtic and Rangers on consecutive Saturdays put Ayr United into second place in the table, five points behind Hearts. This time it was a 2-0 winning margin. Consistent with a common initiative across the land, soldiers in uniform were now being admitted to Somerset Park at half-price. At the Rangers game one officer was spotted paying the admission cost of close to a hundred of his men. (100 at the concessionary price of threepence would have amounted to about £122 in today's money).

Arthur Dale, inside-right for the reserves, enlisted in the Sherwood Foresters. He was a teacher in the Ayr Industrial School. By this time eight players from the junior club Ayr Fort had joined the colours.

A football match took place at Beresford Park between Green's Stars and Ayr Jockeys for the purpose of raising funds to provide cigarettes for the troops. The success was such that enough money was gathered to send 5,000 cigarettes to the theatre of war. This initiative took place at a time when praise was being lashed upon the country's

Jack Lyall - He was a showman in an age in which goalkeepers were seldom inclined to display flamboyancy.

forces for being in the peak of physical condition. During the Boer War the *Ayrshire Post* had carried a cigarette advert for Ogden's. It contained a quote from the esteemed medical journal *The Lancet*. "We are inclined to believe that used with due moderation tobacco is of value second only to food itself." It is worth reading that quote again in order to absorb the conclusion from experts that cigarettes, far from being injurious to health, actually carried health benefits second only to food. In present day society incredulity is regularly summed up by use of the word 'unbelievable'. From the haven of the twenty-first century and without wishing to be accused of writing revisionist history, 'unbelievable' is the right word in this context.

Novelty football may have served its charitable purpose but, in the main, public interest was more heavily attuned to what was happening at Somerset Park. The attraction of a visit from Hearts induced special trains from Edinburgh, Kilmarnock and some of the outlying mining districts. This was a crack Hearts team who were rampant at the top of the league. The fall of Rangers and Celtic at Ayr imbibed confidence that another formidable opponent could be overthrown. A vigorous recruiting effort took place at the match, largely unsuccessful despite the inspiring music discoursed by a large military band. The impulsiveness of recruitment at the outbreak was fading. Perhaps there was a belief that it would soon be over. Continued reports of German retreats and casualties could easily have conveyed that impression. An *Ayrshire Post* headline read: GERMANY'S DOOM AS CERTAIN AS THE FALL OF THE LEAF. This was down to the interpretation of front line intelligence rather than journalistic misadventure. A reluctance to fight might also have originated in people being vigilant enough to scrutinise the fine detail of some of the reports of trench warfare in France. Graphic accounts of machine gun fire, enemy bombs, hand-to-hand fighting and bayonet attacks would have done nothing to inspire anyone of a squeamish sensibility.

Talks took place which had the potential to stall or abandon the start of season 1914/15. Undeterred the season got underway on 15th August, 1914. In searing heat Ayr United beat Partick Thistle 4-0 at Somerset Park. Beforehand the team posed for the camera. Standing - Aitken(trainer), Nevin, Dainty, McLaughlan, Richardson, Goodwin, Lyall. Sitting - Middleton, Cassidy, McStay, Bell, McMillan.

Hearts won 2-0 at Ayr with the following team: Boyd, Crossan, Currie, Briggs, Scott, Mercer, Low, Wattie, Gracie, Graham and Wilson.

James Boyd was fated to die at the Somme on 3rd August, 1916, at the age of twenty-one. Duncan Currie was killed on 1st July, 1916, the first day of the battle of the Somme. Henry Wattie, aged twenty-three at the time, was also killed on that first day of battle. Another Hearts player to die in that battle on that day was Ernie Ellis, albeit he was not in that team at Ayr. Thomas Gracie died from war wounds at the age of twenty-six on 23rd October, 1915.

There was a mass enlistment of Hearts players on 25th November, 1914. Sir George McCrae and Sir James Leishman were forming a new battalion of the Royal Scots and they turned up at Tynecastle Park on that day by arrangement to talk to the Hearts players and staff. Currie, Briggs, Low, Wattie, Gracie and Wilson of the first team volunteered as did Findlay, Frew, Ness, Ellis and Preston of the reserves. Eleven in total; it was a splendid example.

Three days later Ayr United drew 1-1 at Hampden Park in a league fixture, one report eliciting this comment: "There is no football club in Scotland which has been so heavily handicapped as Queen's Park in the matter of the loss of the services of players through the war claims."

Six Falkirk players emulated their Hearts counterparts by joining McCrae's Battalion. One of them was Robert Godfrey whom Ayr United were to purchase from Bathgate for £55 in August 1920. He was the grandfather of Peter Godfrey who was a prominent player with St. Mirren in the 1980s. McCrae's Battalion also attracted six players from Raith Rovers. One week after the Queen's Park match report had touched on the enlistment activity of Ayr United's opponents the theme was revisited when Raith Rovers played at Ayr.

"The appearance in the arena of the Raith Rovers players excited more than the usual interest, the news being fresh of the volunteering of some half-a-dozen recruits for Sir George

Jimmy Richardson scoring in a 2-0 victory at home to Rangers on 17th October, 1914.

McCrae's Edinburgh Battalion. The arrangement whereby these football volunteers are allowed to play in matches for their clubs where at all possible, pleases the public very much."

With complete disinclination towards sentiment the Raith Rovers team received a 3-0 defeat. The military band from Ayr Barracks made its habitual appearance but the recruitment team was being made to work increasingly hard. At the previous home match, versus Morton, the band had marched across the pitch led by Crimean War veteran Sergeant Gaffney, one of only three survivors of that conflict left in the town. By late January 1915 he was one of two. The other was James Clark, the historian of the Royal Scots Fusiliers, a regiment that was shaping history right then. His home, Inkerman Cottage, was named after a famous Crimean battle in which he had fought. At the Raith Rovers game, a zealous recruiting sergeant was heard to offer a cigar and a whisky and soda to anyone who would join the colours.

On 12th December, 1914, Johnny Crosbie's appearance in the Ayr team at Dundee was facilitated by the relative locality of his billet at Cupar (13 miles away). He renewed the acquaintance of the Ayr party at Dundee Station before heading to Dens Park to inflict a 3-2 defeat on the home team, courtesy of a Jimmy Richardson hat-trick. Army training had made a markedly beneficial effect on Crosbie. No longer of such frail build he had put on more than a stone in weight, this despite an illness which had lasted for six weeks. The loud backing accorded by members of the Ayrshire Yeomanry (not to be confused with Crosbie's Lanarkshire Yeomanry) prompted Dundee supporters to form the mistaken impression that a special train had been laid on for the Ayr support.

By now it was truly a war of attrition. A story emerged that the Germans had concocted a plan to retreat from Flanders and fall back all the way to Antwerp. This was palpable nonsense. Both sides were standing their ground in scenes of stalemate and slaughter. Only for one day was there a cessation of hostilities - the famous Christmas truce of 1914. In the field hospitals and trenches, concerts were enjoyed without fear of terror. It was a peaceful interlude. Private H. Kelly, an Ayr man fighting at the front with the 2nd Battalion of the Argyll and Sutherland Highlanders, described the truce in a letter to a colleague at the Ayr Tramways Depot. Please note the Ayr United allegiance declared in the P.S.

"We had a great Christmas Eve. The Germans were shouting over all sorts of good wishes for a Merry Christmas. One of the Germans, who could speak very good English, and who had lived in Glasgow for four years, offered to come out alone from his trench if one of us would meet him half-way, also alone. Well, the sporting offer was accepted, and the two of them met, exchanged greetings and souvenirs. These men were the reserve regiments, and are wishing it was all over. It is the real old Yuletide weather too, Jack Frost being very much in evidence. On Boxing Day the Germans sent over a shell or two by way of a Christmas box, but they didn't do any damage. P.S. See old Ayr are still going great guns. I see also that Dundee still think a lot of Herbert Dainty and Jack Lyall. We have great arguments out here on the results I assure you."

The reference to player-manager Herbert Dainty clearly alludes humorously to the vendetta he still had with his former club Dundee. Goalkeeper Jack Lyall could also list Dundee as a former club although the background to his mention in this context is obscure. Yet no matter the horror of the Western Front it failed to erase thoughts of Ayr United.

"At Greenock, as elsewhere, football patronage has been much affected by the large numbers of supporters who have joined one branch or another of the country's army, so the dimensions of the crowd were somewhat attenuated, the total falling a good bit short of 4,000."

In times of peace this match would have drawn a far bigger crowd. It was played on Boxing Day, a traditionally favourable date for attendances. With Morton sitting third and Ayr United fifth, it had the ingredients of an attractive fixture. Yet the attendance was partially redressed in the observation that:

"With so many soldiers camped in the district they were very well represented at the match, the khaki colour being most pronounced all round the field. Among them were a number of Royal Scots Fusiliers who were glad to renew acquaintance with their Ayr football favourites."

Morton winning 3-0 did not deter the home crowd from barracking Buchanan, their own centre-forward. They were more at ease with the display of their teenaged winger Stan Seymour, whom time would mark as a Newcastle United legend.

The year 1914 was one of catastrophic reflection. The normality of January through to early August had paled into insignificance but the local population had enough resilience to herald 1915 in time-honoured fashion. Shortly before midnight a large crowd gathered at the steeple. The stroke of midnight gave way to some lusty cheering and an outbreak of handshaking. First fittin' expeditions were indulged in. Ayr United had home games on Saturday 2nd January (Third Lanark were beaten) and Monday 4th (Hibs were beaten). The absence of a game on the first was a mercy. "On New Year's Day Jupiter Pluvius did his best to wash Ayr off the planet." That was such a beautiful way to describe something as mundane as a wet winter's day.

The gates were down in comparison with the normal expectancy over a holiday period. Wretched weather was a mitigating factor. The war was another.

Clearly the conclusion was that gates would remain modest until peace was restored. Clubs were beginning to feel the effect financially. Players had been compelled to have the terms of their contracts reduced by 25% but the savings did not equate to nearly as much as the reduction in gate receipts. Contentiously a popular opinion persisted that the discontinuance of football was necessary because it was preventing young men from joining the army. This argument did not entirely lack substance. Men had enlisted in droves but that had not caused the recruitment drive to lose momentum. The opposite was true. It is a fact, rather than a callous observation, that men had also been slaughtered in their droves. With Ayr United going strong why would a man depart these shores to face a high possibility of a grisly death? The best answer to that question is patriotism. Cleverly crafted advertisements and cartoons pricked at the conscience. To phrase it in a blunt term it was emotional blackmail. What had once been obituary columns were no longer mere columns. In retrospect we can all be grateful that we have not had to live through such harrowing times.

In January 1915 the House of Lords debated whether young men should be compelled to join up. The conclusion that there was no need for conscription was tempered by Lord Haldane saying: "If the national stress should become more acute we will bar nothing that may be necessary."

The obvious way to serve the country was by donning khaki but there were other ways. By January 1915, John Bell, the Ayr United right-back, was engaged in Government work in London. Censorship forbade more detail about what he was doing so it had to remain cloaked in intrigue. He continued to make the long journey each weekend to turn out for the club. His effectiveness was noticeably impaired though not sufficiently as to prevent his regular selection.

Disturbingly an obituary had to be written for one of the club's greatest fans.

> "Corporal Donald Macaulay
> Another Ayr man has laid down his life for King and country. On 20th January he died of wounds received in action in No. 2 General Hospital, Le Havre. The sad intelligence was conveyed to his wife, who resides at 31 Weaver Street, Newton-on-Ayr. He was aged thirty. He leaves a widow and two young children, the youngest of whom is thirteen months old. He joined Lord Kitchener's Army towards the end of August. He was attached to the

1st Battalion of the Royal Scots Fusiliers. He was sent to France on 4th December and was about five weeks out when he got wounded and removed to Le Havre.

There was no keener supporter of Ayr United than Macaulay and many football enthusiasts will readily recall his genial personality."

How grim that his survival in trench warfare was equated in weeks.

Another worrying aspect was thrust upon the town of Ayr in relation to shipping traffic. There was a German submarine in the Irish Sea and its presence had the potential for chaos since there was a very large incidence of shipping traffic between Ayr and Irish ports. Shipping was detained in Belfast and, temporarily, there were no arrivals at Ayr from Ireland. There was no suspension of outward sailing. The Admiralty responded by issuing a chilling instruction that steamers could sail at their own risk.

This was part of a German plan to impose starvation on Britain by imposing a blockade to prevent imports of food. In the House of Commons Winston Churchill said: "Britain is to be the object of a kind of warfare never before practised by the civilised world."

The threat of food shortages brought the impact of the war to home shores. People in Ayr had been ridiculed for panic-buying on the day the war had begun. At the time it had seemed a badly impulsive thing to do. Those of a calmer disposition clearly thought that starvation was a most unlikely contingency. Irrational thoughts and actions were clearly not conducive to the war effort yet the underlying fear was not totally misplaced.

The Ayr United team selection for an away game against Partick Thistle might have been described as critical in another time. In January 1915 'critical' had a more clearly defined meaning and was wholly inappropriate to the non-availability of footballers. There was advance notice that

Willie McStay could not turn up. Jack Lyall was "suddenly indisposed". His indisposal was so sudden that the Ayr United party arrived at Firhill without a goalkeeper. Luckily it was known that reserve goalkeeper Sprigger White had travelled to Glasgow to watch the Celtic versus Hearts match. Luckily? What about the matter of finding him in an age long before mobile phone technology? To the bewilderment of an *Ayrshire Post* journalist he was tracked down. "That mysterious galvanic fluid was called into requisition to get on the trail of the custodian and press him into service at Firhill. How the club's emissaries got the hold of White I do not know." As a reader you may be wondering what the mysterious galvanic fluid was. It was a grandiose reference to petrol! His account of a 2-0 defeat was more plainly worded.

With death already rife, John McDonald met his end in unconventional circumstances. As a right-back he had been transferred from Ayr FC to Blackburn Rovers in May 1903. In a succession of moves he then played for Leeds City, Grimsby Town and Queen's Park Rangers. While playing for Queen's Park Rangers he sustained a football injury so serious that it not only ended his career but also left the tenure of his life uncertain. It was hoped that he would be able to survive for a period of years but on 14th March, 1915, he passed away peacefully at his Woolwich home. His mother, who had just arrived from Ayr, was by his bedside. It was all solemn, dignified and heart-rending. On the Western Front it was not remotely so. *Missing presumed dead* regularly meant that there was nothing left to identify. In June 1918 John's brother Archie died in Canada after a long illness. Archie had been a goalkeeper for the olden-day Ayr FC pending his transfer to Partick Thistle. That left Hugh as the only survivor of the three brothers. He too had been an Ayr FC goalkeeper and his career had included Woolwich Arsenal.

The Ayr players on active service so far were Johnny Crosbie, John Bellringer, Neil McBain, John Hood and Arthur Dale. A further eight were engaged in Government

Willie McStay - Loaned from Celtic from November 1912 until the summer of 1916.

work. Queen's Park had twenty-six players on active service and Hearts had sixteen. The expression 'active service' did not necessarily mean that they had already experienced the dubious thrill of mud and bullets but, if they had not, they were being trained for that eventuality. After a 2-1 win at Airdrie on 17th April, Crosbie's new-found physique was favourably commented upon: "Bronzed and hardy looking, he isn't like the youngster we used to admire at Somerset Park and the military training seems to have done him a power of good."

As the 1914/15 season drew to a close the Ayr United board publicly acknowledged the services of the ladies who had assisted in the collections for the various war funds. The accumulated total from Somerset Park and Beresford Park topped £200. Relief funds were the priority though, in another gesture, the club had donated forty-two footballs to the forces.

A fifth-placed finish was very close to being bettered. Fourth place was denied only by Morton's superior goal average. Jimmy Richardson tied for the honour of being the top scorer in the First Division. Together with Thomas Gracie of Hearts he scored twenty-nine. A pedantic analysis of the statistics would have favoured the Ayr man, who played in thirty-seven games as opposed to Gracie, who played in all thirty-eight. In the grand scheme of things goalscoring ratios were of derisory significance. By October of that year Gracie had sacrificed his life for King and country. Richardson would not survive the war unscathed though he was to get through the ordeal with his life intact.

In the financial year extending from 1st April, 1914, until 31st March, 1915, the club made a loss of £448 : 5s : 11½d. At the close of the previous financial year the credit balance had sat at £396 : 3s : 11½d. The arithmetic will tell you that this left a debit balance of £52 : 2s.

The shareholders who congregated at the Y.M.C.A. Hall to hear those figures delivered were small in number. Mr Charles Gray, presiding, had a plentiful stock of mitigating factors.

"At the beginning of last season our prospects were very bright. We held a very high position on the league table, our players were keen and full of enthusiasm, the balance at the bank was on the right side, and situated as we are in a town and district famous for their patronage to sport, we had good reason to believe a brilliant season was before us. Owing to the great European War, however, into which we were plunged, our business suffered in common with others; we were faced with a time of exceptional difficulty and abnormal conditions, and I think you will agree with me that this report, considering all these circumstances, is a very satisfactory one in every way. There has been a good deal of controversy as to whether it was right and proper to carry on the game during the present crisis. Whatever the merits of the case for or against, I would like to remind you that our president (Tom Steen) was one of the deputation who visited the War Office to ascertain the attitude of the authorities on this important subject, and it was only on their advice that we decided to continue. Meantime we are in a state of suspension, and rightly so, and what the immediate future has in store for us, it would not be wise to prophesy. The business of the year has entailed on those in charge a very considerable amount of labour and anxiety, but I can assure you that my brother directors have not spared themselves in looking after the interests of the club. Especially we are indebted to our chairman, Mr Steen, who by his long experience of the game is so thoroughly fitted to control the very considerable negotiations which devolve on a company such as ours. I would also add a word of thanks to our genial and energetic secretary – Mr Gemson – who combines in a very exceptional degree all the qualities that go to make an ideal official. We have been able to forward a considerable sum of money, and, among other articles, a large number of footballs – these being in continual demand from supporters of our team in France. We retain – with one exception – all our players on our list, and no transfers have been made."

In May 1915 the Jockey Club abandoned racing, with the exception of the Newmarket meetings, for the duration. The historic Epsom Derby therefore did not take place for the first time since the inaugural event 135 years earlier. The Jockey Club was precipitated towards this radical action at the request of the Government. A powerful lobby sought the discontinuance of football. The case for discontinuance was strong. The default counter argument was the game's usefulness for raising money for charitable institutions. A state of virtual apoplexy was reached by the anti-football lobby, not without justification.

Consider the ordeal suffered by a Mrs Ruth Logan. She was sailing from New York to Liverpool on the Lusitania when it was sunk by a U-boat on 7th May, 1915. The German embassy in Washington DC had placed warnings in American newspapers. Bearing no scope for doubt, prospective passengers were told that any ship flying a British flag, or that of any of Britain's allies, would be a potential target. When the ship was struck by an enemy torpedo it went down in eighteen minutes and 1,195 of the 1,959 on board perished. Mrs Logan survived but in all the chaos she lost her grip on her two-year-old son and he drowned. The relevance of telling this story here is that the lady's address was 6 Tryfield Place, Ayr. She lived in one of the tenement flats right opposite Somerset Park. An abundance of local people had similarly tragic stories. Some had lost more than one son in the war. Yet we can only guess at the impact on an emotionally scarred mind when the football legions continued to make their way to matches played right in front of that lady's flat. Her husband was on active service in the 1st Gordon Highlanders and there was always the added fear of receiving a dreaded communication from the War Office. Football, with its attendant emotions, hardly had a moral case against abandonment quite apart from the practical considerations of war work.

On 23rd May, 1915, Italy declared war on Austria-Hungary. Inevitably Germany then declared war on Italy. The course of the hostilities was turning into a conflagration, especially when we factor in the fighting against the Turks in the Dardanelles and the assistance of troops from Australia and New Zealand (Anzacs) in that campaign.

Morally indefensible though football was, there was no shortage of volunteers for military service. By the summer of 1915 more men were forthcoming than the military system could handle. This made a mockery of the unceasing campaign for conscription. Arguing against the need for conscription someone suggested in the *Ayrshire Post* that: "The voluntary principle has justified itself fully and given us the very pick of the nation's manhood."

In the pioneering years of football in Ayr a prominent name was William Beveridge. In 1879 he played for Scotland against England and Wales at a time when his club team was Ayr Academy. In 1880, by now at university, he was chosen to play against Wales again. Not until 1965 did an Ayr Academy former pupil next play for Scotland. That was Ian Ure. Beveridge was an outstanding athlete too. Reputedly he could give long starts in handicap races and still win easily. By 1915 he was the Rev. Colonel W. W. Beveridge of Princes Street U. F. Church, Port Glasgow. In that capacity he was chaplain to the Royal Scots Fusiliers stationed at Fort Matilda in Greenock. The War Office instructed him to hold himself in readiness to proceed to the front. When the call came he was despatched to the theatre of war although, as a chaplain, he was not required to brandish a gun. This immunity from killing did not prevent him from entering dangerous areas as illustrated by a letter to his congregation which began:

> "It was a tragic moment that I reached the front. The Germans had, a few hours before, committed their crowning gas atrocity before Ypres. Determined to force back the wedge driven by the British Army into their line, the enemy employed poison fumes to a far greater extent than in any former attack. Several miles away from the trenches I felt the presence of gas, which

made the eyes smart and water. The attack had been delivered in the night, under cover of darkness."

The logistical difficulties of dealing with recruitment levels threatened to intensify when Lord Kitchener said that he wanted another 300,000 men. There was a height restriction of not less than 5' 2" and an age range of nineteen to forty. The Ayrshire Territorial Force Association was tasked with providing 2,500 men. Ayr, Irvine and Kilmarnock had recruiting stations. "Recruits will be clothed, equipped, and start training at once" was strongly indicative of a level of urgency. The mobilisation of so much manpower had to be a consideration when a joint conference of the Football League, Scottish League, Irish League and Southern League was held in the boardroom of the Blackpool Winter Gardens in July. If so, it was an insufficient consideration. In a unified display of intransigence the decision to continue was endorsed.

As a follow-on from the Blackpool meeting, the Scottish Football League First Division committee convened a meeting in Glasgow and the following points were passed.

- In any football which the League may carry on during 1915/16, no player shall be engaged unless such player is regularly employed throughout the week during the term of his engagement in work other than football or in connection with football, and no club shall allow its interests to interfere with the work of players engaged in Government work.
- The guarantee to be paid to visiting clubs is to be reduced to £30.
- The maximum wage to be paid to all players shall be £1 per match played by the club.
- No football will be played except on Saturdays or holidays.
- The latest hour of kick-off shall be 4 o'clock instead of 3.30 as formerly.

The compulsion to engage in non-football-related work would already have been ingrained in the conscience of Ayr

United players anyway. During the 1915 close season winger Billy Middleton returned to his Tyneside roots to work in the shipyards of Palmers of Jarrow.

Goalkeeper Jack Lyall headed in the same direction. He went to live in Newcastle where he found work as a plasterer. Whereas Middleton was to return for the new season, Lyall had played his last game for the club. He next played for Jarrow, the club he had represented back at the start of a fabulous career in which he won the Football League title with Sheffield Wednesday (1902/03 and 1903/04), the F.A. Cup with Sheffield Wednesday (1907) and the Second Division title with Manchester City (1909/10). As a further distinction he played for Scotland against England in 1905. Throughout it all he was a great showman.

Prolific striker Jimmy Richardson got fixed-up with work at the carpet factory of W.C. Gray and Sons just a short distance from Somerset Park. This may have been construed as a soft option but trench warfare would eventually be his lot.

Hilly (Alex Hill) Goodwin, who had been with the club since scoring twice on his debut on 1st April, 1911, joined the 14th Argyll and Sutherland Highlanders. He was to survive the war, eventually passing away at the age of fifty-seven on 26th September, 1948. Some players of his acquaintance died within days of each other. Former Ayr United goalkeeper Sam Herbertson was killed on 12th July, 1915, while in action with the Royal Scots Fusiliers in the Dardanelles. He was aged twenty-six. John Bellringer, one of the club's reserve players, was killed in action in the same location on the same day. He was aged twenty-three and serving with the Argyll and Sutherland Highlanders. Both of them have their names commemorated on the Helles Memorial, Turkey. Two days later Bob Capperauld, also of Ayr United reserves, died. As with Sam Herbertson he had been with the Royal Scots Fusiliers in the Dardanelles. He was removed to a hospital in Alexandria after being wounded. His father received a communication to that effect at his home in Ayr's Elba Street.

Hilly (Alex Hill) Goodwin. He survived active service in the Great War and lived until the age of fifty-seven.

The next communication carried the news that the wounds were fatal. Harry Simpson, an ex-Ayr United forward, survived the wounds he suffered while fighting the Turks in the Dardanelles. He too was one of the Royal Scots Fusiliers. Hugh McBride, formerly a reserve player, was hospitalised in Malta after being wounded in that same theatre of war. His brother John was to die at the Somme while serving with the Black Watch on 14th December, 1916. Peter, an elder brother of theirs, was a goalkeeper who was sold by Ayr FC to Preston North End in December 1895 and he remained with them until the end of 1911/12.

"The carrying on of the game at all, with the European war raging fiercely, has brought forth condemnatory protests in many quarters. It may happen that the course of the war will render necessary a stoppage of football, but it is to be hoped that Great Britain and her allies will soon succeed in choking off the German Huns and those associated with them."

This statement did more than merely allude to the possibility that the game might be halted. Yet in the same newspaper there was an advertisement for Ayr United season tickets priced at 7s 6d for adults and three shillings for juveniles. Keeping going was placing clubs in varying degrees of difficulty. For instance nine of Beith's players were in the forces and so was the majority of their committee. At First Division level player availability was going to be a more acute problem than before. That was because a good number of those who had enlisted were still available to play for their clubs in 1914/15, at least on a sporadic basis. Broadly speaking the scale of appearances was consistent with the proximity of the locality where their regiment was stationed. By August 1915 most of the regiments had mobilised and were already at their war stations. Ayr United, in common with other clubs, also had players engaged in Government work. The clandestine connotation should not convey the message that this work was glamorous. If it was in the field of munitions work it was apt to be mundane and dangerous. Irrespective of what it entailed, the war effort was now dictating that a lot of Government work had to be carried out on Saturdays and Sundays.

To flout what was required in terms of the war effort was to risk the disfavour of the Defence of the Realm Act (known as DORA). This was a catch-all piece of legislation aimed at criminalising anything deemed to be prejudicial to the national interest. Extreme contraventions such as spying incurred facing a firing squad. Sedition was dealt with in accordance with the scale of the severity. People strolling across Ayr's Low Green on the Sunday evening of 15th August, 1915, would have heard a speaker in full flow. He was a Glasgow teacher called James Blair Houston. During his address he made the following points.

- As a nation Great Britain loves war more than peace.
- By preparing for war in times of peace Britain has brought this war on itself.
- The present war is desired and caused by capitalists who are deriving pecuniary benefit.
- No woman wants her sons to enlist in His Majesty's Forces.
- Anyone who enlists in His Majesty's Forces is a fool.

Under the Defence of the Realm Act Houston appeared at Ayr Sheriff Court where he had a £10 fine imposed.

Clydeside revolutionary John MacLean remains the best remembered of Scotland's anti-war campaigners, eventually going to jail for his principles. Whereas MacLean's name passed into Scottish folklore, Houston's found obscurity even although his arrest for sedition in Ayr came two months before MacLean's first brush with the law.

Bitterness about the international situation was understandable but restraint had to be exercised in the manner in which these emotions were manifested. An objective social commentator would have admitted that public morale was wavering yet to admit as much on a public platform was tantamount to inviting arrest. The tragic overtones of the time were most evident to the Ayr United party on arrival at Dundee for the first match of season 1915/16.

After the train had pulled in their attention was immediately drawn to a Red Cross train on an adjacent platform. It had brought more than ninety wounded men from Southampton. A fleet of ambulances was at the scene to convey these men to the infirmary and the Ayr party watched while the last one departed. The effect was visible. Whatever level of enthusiasm there had been was now evaporated. Switcher McLaughlan was absent - he missed his train at his native Kilwinning. In the subsequent rehash of the team, club trainer Sanny Aitken appeared at outside-right at Dens Park that day. His experience as a player was back in the days of the old Ayr FC and he was now aged 42 years 136 days. This made him the oldest player to make a competitive appearance for Ayr United. The record was threatened on 15th November, 1997, when goalkeeper Henry Smith appeared at the age of 41 years 250 days. Coincidentally this was at the same Dens Park venue. The record now belongs to Alan Main, who made three appearances for the club, culminating in a match at Alloa on 11th September, 2010, when he was aged 42 years 280 days.

In losing 2-0 to Dundee, the opening goal was scored by Alec Troup who was making his debut after signing from Forfar Athletic. His career was to extend to 1933 during which time he also played for Everton and Scotland. There will be more about 'Wee Troupie' on a further page since he was to guest for Ayr United.

"The homeward journey was begun at 7 o'clock, and at that time the scene at the station was vastly different from that which we witnessed on our arrival in the forenoon. At night our train was weighted with the responsibility of carrying two newly-wedded couples – both bridegrooms being soldiers, and of all the showers of confetti we have ever seen, the Dundee display beat it hollow. The piles of small paper discs lay so thick on the platform and in the compartment that one could have stooped down and lifted a 'gowffin-fu' quite easily. The Ayr contingent of the party did not get home till after 12 o'clock."

Switcher McLaughlan - His trade absented him from the call of the Great War.

This summary could leave us to contemplate the meaning of 'gowffin-fu' but rather than dwell on the Scottish vernacular it would be more appropriate to focus on the reference to both grooms being soldiers. Did they survive the killing fields they were destined for?

The first home match of the season was a 3-2 loss against Hibs. At the kick-off time barely two thousand people were in Somerset Park. The numbers were then greatly enhanced by a late rush. It was a wet day so were the latecomers waiting on a dry spell pending a dash to the match? No! In fact dry was just about the least likely word to be used in their vocabulary. Increased hours created by the national emergency at least had the compensation of correspondingly higher wages. To the Government it was a cause for concern that the war effort was in danger of being impeded by the fact that much of the additional disposable income was being spent on alcohol. And it was a fact rather than something drawn from mere opinion. It was a boom time for the nation's pubs; a hangover was far from conducive to working in a munitions factory for example. Prohibition would have been draconian. As a compromise the opening hours were limited. So when Ayr United were kicking-off against Hibs the opening of the local pubs was, by law, synchronised with the start of the match. The farcical consequence was that men were seen queuing outside pubs to wait on the doors opening. A stampede towards the bar preceded a swift drink then a hasty departure for the match (or what was left of it). Weather conditions ensured that they were wet on the outside and wet on the inside. Readers may well be contemplating that the inconvenience of it all could have been foregone in favour of deferring the pub visit until later. This would take no cognisance of the tribal ritual undergone by supporters since the game's pioneering years. To many it is part of the fabric of the match day experience.

Billy Middleton's temporary exclusion was on account of him having had no time for training since his arrival back from Tyneside. Johnny Crosbie's imminent departure for foreign service told of an impending absence of a more permanent nature.

In keeping with football's shred of moral justification a charity match was contested at Beresford Park between Ayr United and the 3rd Glasgow Highlanders. The proceeds were split between the Glasgow Highlanders and the local Territorials' funds. It was an even match with the Ayr team being below strength and the military side being composed mainly of senior players. The 'sodgers' won 5-4. Opportunities to do the right thing continued to be seized upon. On the last Saturday in September the team played out a 1-1 draw amidst vile weather in Aberdeen. Two wounded soldiers from Ayr were known to be laid up in an Aberdeen hospital and some of the Ayr party took the time to visit them. On the next away trip pity was a scarce commodity when Jimmy Richardson scored a hat-trick in a 5-0 rout at Tynecastle Park. The word pity is used in the context of an observation that: "No club in Scotland has been as hard hit as the Heart of Midlothian in the matter of the loss of players who have gone on military service." Yet the vanquished Hearts team could hardly have been defined as being bereft of ability. At the time of the return league engagement in January they were second in the league, although the undaunted Ayr team succeeded in beating them again (3-1).

In the autumn of 1915 the western campaign was characterised by intense artillery combats and a succession of fierce attacks by the Germans who were attempting to recover lost positions. The Allies fighting the Turks in the Dardanelles had it similarly tough. Casualty lists were obscenely long in relation to both theatres of war. One of the names on them was that of Harry Murray, Ayr United's original secretary. After relinquishing that post he was succeeded by Lawrence Gemson. This allowed him to channel his energy into fulfilling his role as a clerk in the commissary department at the County Buildings in Ayr. Not long after the outbreak of war he enlisted in the newly formed Collingwood Battalion of the Royal Naval Division and was posted to England. When his clerical qualifications became known he was drafted into the paymaster's department. A nice clerical job would have been a safe and easy way of seeing out the war. Would have been! On the night of Monday, 10th May, 1915, he sailed for the Dardanelles and if ever a place could be likened to Armageddon this was it. By getting back out of that place with his life intact he was lucky. He got wounded and was admitted to a hospital in Malta early in September. To aid his recovery he was shipped back home for a time of recuperation and was fit enough to travel with the Ayr United party for a fixture at Airdrie on 13th November. Airdrie winning 3-1 was not even a close contender for Harry Murray's greatest trauma of 1915.

Following on from the Airdrie match, right-half George Getgood played two more games for Ayr United before he left in mysterious circumstances. At the age of twenty-two in August 1915, the Coylton-born Getgood signed for the club, his previous club being Reading. He was a very good player and, for a visit from Celtic in December, his inclusion on the team list was automatic. On the morning of the match a letter was received by John Bell, the team captain. Getgood's epistle explained that he had left for London. Doctor's orders compelled Jack Nevin to be a late call-off "thus was the fine edifice of a new formation brought to a clatter." Justification for such poetic licence was a 4-0 loss. Getgood's written explanation of his absence did not expand to state any specific reasons although he did resurface in the team lists of his former club Reading where he became a team mate of another ex-Ayr United player, Joe Cassidy. Why the seemingly impulsive flight from Ayr? Speculatively it may be suggested that it could have been prompted for reasons of military service. He was already an ex-Royal Scots Fusilier and in April 1916 he enlisted in the Royal Army Medical Corps. By a considerable period he survived the war, dying in Kidderminster on 22nd July, 1970, at the age of seventy-seven. He had settled there with his family, his affinity to that area dating to his time playing for Kidderminster Harriers. At the peak of his career he captained Wolves.

Billy Middleton's decision to join the Ayrshire Yeomanry foretold the non-availability of another quality player.

Certain developments within the war had the effect of stiffening public resolve in a more effective manner than even the most zealous of recruitment campaigns could. The sinking of the *Lusitania* was one such. The execution of Edith Cavell on 12th October, 1915, was another. She was an English nurse working in enemy-occupied Belgium and she tended to the wounded of both sides. Heroically she played a part in assisting allied soldiers to escape from the country. Discovery of her actions was a prospective risk to her life. The risk materialised and she was executed by firing squad while still wearing her nurse's uniform. In terms of propaganda the ramifications of it were huge. Sensing national and international revulsion her martyrdom was used to intensify hatred of the enemy. This episode consolidated the vilification of the Germans and was doubtlessly influential in prompting some men to give up the comforts of home and take up arms. Coincidentally, the Government had just begun to address the problem of the diminishing flow of recruits.

On the day before the execution of Edith Cavell, Lord Derby was empowered to take charge of recruitment. The scheme he came up with was called the Group Scheme, though it was popularly referred to as the Derby Scheme. Whatever the guise it was based on a simple premise. Men aged between eighteen and forty could still volunteer or, as a compromise, they could attest. Attestation meant that they were giving an undertaking to be called up when required. If they volunteered for immediate service they were categorised as Class B. The class A men went about their normal daily lives until receiving the call-up. Registration under the Group Scheme had a deadline date of 15th December, 1915. That date was a Wednesday and, on the weekend prior, there was chaos in Ayr. A late rush of men besieged the various recruitment centres which were crowded all day, right up until a late hour. Officials struggled to cope with it all and such scenes were replicated all over Britain. Conscription was imminent and these men knew it. This way they could choose which branch of the forces to join.

On the Saturday before Christmas Ayr United lost 1-0 away to St. Mirren in frosty conditions that rendered the pitch hard. Still, it was insignificantly cold in Paisley. Insignificant, that is, in comparison to the cold winter being endured in the Dardanelles. Lieutenant Campbell of the Ayrshire Yeomanry had this to say in a letter.

"The 28th November was something to be remembered, and was our first real taste of what a winter campaign in a barren and flat country can mean. The procession to the trenches that morning was like being on a polar expedition – and we arrived there like snowmen. As the blizzard kept on and the temperature went well below freezing point next night, life in open trenches was just the limit of what one would imagine people could endure."

On Christmas Day Kilmarnock were beaten 2-0 at Ayr. With so many men on active service the crowd numbered between four and five thousand. This was conservatively several thousand below what might have been expected in times of peace. The seasonal joy combined with the result should have made it an ultra happy day. Should have! An *Ayrshire Post* scribe put his own slant on it.

"The time was when Christmastide was associated with merriment. Even the most casual glance around sufficed to dispel any idea that Christmas Day itself was anything else than a tragedy. From the firing line in the west came the familiar story of howitzers roaring in their lairs, of the air filled with the dolorous cries of tearing shot and shell, of men existing in the very jaws of death in the unspeakably muddy and weary trenches."

Ayr United had a rampant start to 1916. After drawing 2-2 against Queen's Park at Hampden on New Year's Day, wins were recorded against Dumbarton (3-1), Clyde (2-0), Hearts

(3-1) Morton (0-1) and Queen's Park again (4-1). With eleven points taken from a possible twelve what could be wrong with the world? This is intended to be a leading question. There was a great deal wrong with the world. The *Ayrshire Post* column denigrating Christmas was trumped by that newspaper's even franker assessment of the New Year. A heading of A BLACK NEW YEAR sat atop a column carrying this less than inspiring, though realistic, summary.

"Not within living memory has the New Year season been passed under more depressing auspices. Nature herself did nothing to lighten the gloom. Her contribution was storm and rain, and all manner of unpleasantness. She was, in fact, thoroughly emblematic in her trying varieties of discomfort of the conditions that obtained in the world at large. The war itself is chronic. It is not a day to day event. It must needs be looked upon with the long vision. It has rolled on its grievous way like a snowball, gathering as it has gone, until it has embraced not only all the slaughtering devices that are known to the wit of man, and rendering it the more absolutely needful, in the interest of common humanity, that the present Armageddon should have its issue in a war upon war as a necessary preventative to a world lapse back into the crudest ways of a barbarism that is the more savage and barbaric in the ratio of its own scientific developments, but all the economic factors that are in effect the lives of men, women and children. The war must go on to many a bitter end. The year came in with many expressions of the assurance that eventually all will be well. Reigning monarchs, heads of States, Governments, Armies – all the individual and consolidated might of the allied cause had the same message, and from every quarter came the same note of unshaken determination and abounding confidence. Nothing more can be said than that the issue remains where it was a year ago. What looms up is many a hard-fought field and much shedding of blood, and behind the gory outcomes of many fierce fights, untold sufferings and numberless sorrows."

That was the Happy New Year message 1916-style! It highlights a misconception that press censorship was always used to suppress feelings of discontent in war time Britain. Assurances of grounds for optimism are ridiculed and it concludes with a prediction of impending misery. The source of that misery would no longer be the Dardanelles. The attack had begun on 21st February, 1915. After a momentous decision to withdraw, the last of the allied troops were evacuated on 7th January, 1916. The former Ayr United players Sam Herbertson, John Bellringer and Bob Capperauld had failed to survive a battle culminating in defeat. Was there any need to fight in the Dardanelles? The motive was the dual purpose of eliminating Turkey from the war and opening up a trade route with our Russian allies.

Punctuating football reports with war references was a natural tendency. In winning 1-0 at Morton's Cappielow Park, Ayr United gathered the two points after recourse to extensive defending. This brought forth a comment to the effect that: "The result of the contest is a testimonial to the Ayr United defence, and, as has been demonstrated on the European battlefield, the most persistent attackers often come off second best." The battlefield analogy threatened to resonate with players and spectators alike. After the match fans would have had ample time to dwell on any analogies. It was documented that: "The Greenock tramway cars don't break any speed records. Returning from Cappielow, many passengers came off and walked."

In that same month of January 1916, the Military Service Bill was introduced. In effect it was the introduction of the much dreaded conscription. Men aged eighteen to forty-one were liable to be called up for military service. If anyone felt that they had grounds for exemption they could apply to a local tribunal by 2nd March. Those who were medically unfit had an obvious case for exemption as had ministers of religion. The grey areas were in respect of essential wartime occupations and conscientious objectors. How essential was the occupation? Were the principles of pacifism enough to justify avoiding the call-up?

This development ignited predictable recruiting campaigns. The crux of these campaigns was to get the message over that men should join up while they could still choose their own battalion. Delay would see them conscripted to a branch of the armed forces of someone else's choosing. An urgent wire was sent to the Provost of Ayr from Lord Derby.

"I would respectfully beg you to do all in your power to induce men, especially single men, to join the Army under the group system. It is still open for voluntary enlistment, and I am anxious that as many as possible should take advantage before the Military Service Bill becomes operative. The Lord Mayor of London has, with excellent results, opened a special recruiting office in the Mansion House and has himself appealed to the young men of the metropolis. Would it be too much to ask you, if it is not already being done, to do the same in your city [sic] in consultation with the local recruiting committee?"

The Ayr Burgh Tribunal sat frequently to listen to a proliferation of appeals to be excused military service. A common argument was that the absence of key personnel could put a business at risk of collapsing. Certain cases received a sympathetic hearing and other cases were treated with nothing short of sheer derision.

Trench warfare had no redeeming features. Quite apart from the obvious chance of death, the trenches were ridden with mud, rats and fleas. The opportunity for recreation was understandably seized upon with great fervour. In March 1916 Private W. Dunlop of the Royal Scots Fusiliers sent a letter from the front. It was addressed to the *Ayrshire Post*. In it he appealed to Ayr United to send "an old football or two." Thoughtfully he qualified his request with "if you have any to spare." His letter also appealed for "thick black tobacco" though, as far as can be ascertained, this part of his appeal was not directed at Ayr United!

The Battle of Verdun had begun on 21st February. Military analysts would eventually look back on this battle and define it as fighting for the sake of fighting, there being a severe lack of justification for the huge casualties on both sides. The combatants were the French and, of course, the Germans but the progress of the battle was of great interest to the British. Progress! Perhaps this is not the best word to use in any context relating to this battle. By March it was described as a holocaust.

Verdun should have been well beyond even the most tenuous of comparisons with a football match. Yet we cannot be so dismissive of football's propensity for the abnormal. When Ayr United arrived at Shawfield to play Clyde on 18th March, 1916, the scene most definitely did fall under the definition of abnormal. It was described as: "A bleak looking enclosure without a grand stand, only part of the foundations remaining of the old structure that was burned down. What at first appeared to be a contractor's pay hut was actually the press facility. It was occupied by five reporters, two telegraph messenger boys and two telephones. The four chairs were occupied and one reporter got a partial seat on a four-inch wooden strap. The others had to stand and all were packed in like the proverbial herring in a barrel." However the actual comparison with the grand battle was in relation to the match, rather than the remnants of a burned-down stand thus far unreplaced. 1-0 down at half-time, Ayr United fought back to score three times in the last twenty minutes to win 3-1. Yes, fought back. The terminology is correct since it was documented that: "There was not much to get enthusiastic about till the United began their supreme effort, which latter had greater success than that of C.P. Willie's has had at Verdun."

Abbreviations were commonly used in war reporting and it is known that C.P. stood for command post. Willie is a clear reference to Kaiser Wilhelm. Piecing this together, the cryptic message being conveyed by the journalist becomes clear. In his analogical way he was telling his readers that Ayr United's late offensive was more successful than that of any German offensive manoeuvres at Verdun. Even with no name appended to the report, the assumption that the reporter was male is 100% safe. Political correctness did not inhabit the world of 1916. Earlier that month a meeting of the Ayr Tramways committee had moved that women drivers could be employed but this was just a concession to absolute necessity. The same necessity compelled women to work in the hitherto male domain of Ayr Gasworks.

At inside-right against Clyde was a player called "Smith". He was described as "an old friend with a new name." Such were the vagaries of war time censorship. Yet censorship was not so strict as to conceal the snippet that former Ayr United players Billy Middleton and Joe Cassidy had formed a right-wing partnership in an army match at Aldershot.

For a match with Third Lanark a week later he was still listed as "Smith" but the Somerset Park crowd would easily have known the identity of the "old friend". In a 6-0 win he scored twice. It comprised the club's biggest First Division victory to that date. The result was superb considering that the opposition goalkeeper was the great Jimmy Brownlie.

The main focus of public interest remained Verdun. Then there was the matter of the U-boat menace. Merchant shipping was being destroyed on a daily basis. Inevitably the cost of living went up, though in mentioning this there is no intention to minimise the far greater cost in human sacrifice. It was a problem accentuated in the North Sea. Prior to the twentieth century the stretch of water now known as the North Sea was called the German Ocean. Hostility between Britain and Germany put the British people ill at ease with the German connotations, hence the change of name.

The modern trend of foreign footballers in the Scottish game was not part of the psyche one hundred years ago. Had it been, there would have been a logistical difficulty surrounding foreign players arriving to play at Ayr. Ayr was named as a restricted area under the Aliens Restrictions Order, 1916.

Aliens could only enter the area with the permission of the registration officer. Even then they had to be in possession of an identity book. Why was Ayr named as a restricted area? The question is easily answered. Merchant shipping plied its trade from the harbour. Espionage was a genuine fear rather than some figment of a fertile imagination.

With conscription underway the local tribunal, which listened to appeals for exemption, struggled to cope with the growing number of cases before them. It was so bad that the South Ayrshire military representative on the tribunal decided to resign citing that the work was too heavy. Some men made themselves into fugitives in order to escape army service.

The country was in a state of high alert. In peace time a group of men alighting from a train at New Cumnock Station would have aroused no suspicion. One group got arrested while camping out in the hills nearby. Among them was a Londoner who had been given a time and place to report for the army but he fled to what he considered to be a remote location. The fugitives were apprehended pending an appearance at Ayr Sheriff Court. The police then handed them over to the army and their £2 fine was deducted from their army pay.

Men camped out in the hills near Carsphairn were arrested in similar circumstances. That group included natives of Wales, Bristol and London. They appeared at Kirkcudbright Sheriff Court.

What were these men afraid of? In truth there was a substantial amount to be afraid of. Under a headline of A BLOODY SUNDAY one newspaper account of battle began: "The details of the Sunday battle at Verdun (9th April, 1916) would make gruesome reading if it were not that the world has within the last year and a half supped so full of horrors that the tragedies of the war have almost come to pass before the vision like the phantom scenes in a cinema hall." Observant readers will have picked up on the point that the allied cause was being fought by the French rather than the British at

Verdun. That much was true but the scenes there were being replicated at Ypres where the British forces were engaging in major assaults to gain small distances.

It virtually defied belief that the Scottish Football Association continued to debate trivia. At a meeting of their Council, the most important item on the agenda was an application by the Scottish Football League for permission to play undated fixtures and postponed league matches on evenings between April 10th and April 30th, provided that the hour of kick-off be not earlier than 6.30 p.m This was unanimously agreed to. Permission was then given for clubs to play matches in midweek and on Saturdays between 1st May and 15th May for recognised charities. Sanction was also given to the Scottish Football League to organise matches on May 20th on behalf of war relief funds.

The contingency plan for clearing a fixtures backlog was expressly stated. So what was the reason for the chaos that ensued on Saturday, 15th April? On that afternoon Ayr United won 3-0 at Fir Park in what was the club's first ever league win at Motherwell. The argument that the Ayr team could have done without a goalkeeper was not open to challenge. One report of the first goal was beautifully characteristic of the art of a football writer in 1916: "Jackson, with a characteristic lunge, got his cranium to the sphere and directed it into the net." The team got great vocal encouragement and the fourth-placed league position was maintained. A wearisome response to defeat has traditionally been: "There's always next week." For Motherwell this psychology did not fit. Having played Ayr United in the afternoon they then had to play Celtic in the evening, again in the league. As a saving grace they again had home advantage. Besides, Celtic had also contested a league fixture in the afternoon. They had beaten Raith Rovers 6-0 at Celtic Park. Motherwell completed their day by losing 3-1 to Celtic. Joe Cassidy, ex-Ayr United, played for Celtic in the evening match, though not in the afternoon. By the following week he was playing for Reading.

There was a further eccentricity in the scheduling on 15th April, 1916. Kilmarnock beat Hearts 3-1 in a league fixture played at Somerset Park whilst Rugby Park was being used for Cattle Show purposes. Since then Kilmarnock have played one more league match at Somerset Park. That was on 26th January, 1946, when they beat Partick Thistle 2-1.

There was a hint of prophecy in the suggestion that Ayr United did not need a goalkeeper at Motherwell. If only that could have been true of future matches. Gordon Kerr, the regular custodian, became Private Kerr of the Gordon Highlanders and was stationed at Aberdeen. Yet by a quirk of luck he was abnormally fortunate in getting generous leave granted and he continued to guard the Ayr United goal until the turn of the year.

Running a football club at this time was ridden with difficulty. With the season drawing to a close, the end could not come quickly enough for those involved. Clubs were able to cobble together a line-up of eleven players but a diminishing availability often meant that teams were short of full strength. With conscription now being ensconced in law, the outlook threatened to get a great deal worse. As if to illustrate how many good players were at the front, a match was played 300 yards behind the firing line. The teams represented 'A' Company Royal Scots Fusiliers and the personnel from their Headquarters. It took place dangerously close to rifle and shell fire. A report of the contest was as detailed as a match report would have been back home. The spectators were the officers and men from the adjacent dugouts.

In the conventional world of football Ayr United entered the season's final league day knowing that fourth place would be secured if Celtic were to beat Partick Thistle and Falkirk were to get nothing better than a draw at Ayr. Partick Thistle proceeded to lose 5-0 at Celtic Park and Ayr United crushed Falkirk 4-1 so fourth place was easily consolidated. This remains a club record. The team's success did not deter a somewhat chequered report at the annual general meeting.

"The continuance of the great European war has had its effect on the finances of the club, the withdrawal of so many of the club's ardent and enthusiastic followers, away at their country's call, reducing the size of the gates and depleting our income by £1,467 : 18s : 6d. The playing strength of the team has been well maintained, and, in spite of the financial strain, a credit balance is the result of the year's working. The war has claimed its victims from amongst our players. Lance Corporal John Bellringer, Argyll and Sutherland Highlanders, and Private Robert Capperauld, Royal Scots Fusiliers, both in the club's service last year, and Private Samuel Herbertson, Royal Scots Fusiliers, who assisted the club on entry in First League circles, paying the supreme price for devotion to their country. We desire to express our deep gratitude to our patrons who so liberally supported the collections at the ground, by means of which £137 : 1s : 2d was gathered for the various war charities. 22,000 cigarettes were despatched to the Royal Scots Fusiliers at the Dardanelles, and seventy footballs, besides jerseys, and flag day donations given to the various arms of the service. Again we are pleased to place on record our appreciation of the wholehearted enthusiasm and earnestness of our players, which has been attended with so much success and made us quite an attraction on other enclosures. The income for the year amounted to £3,271 : 11s : 7d and the expenditure £3,128 : 16s : 2d., leaving a gain on the season's workings of £142 : 15s : 5d."

The annual general meeting of the Scottish Football Association lasted for seven minutes. It was the shortest in their history. After re-electing their office bearers the meeting resolved itself into an extraordinary general meeting.

Kilmarnock 1 Ayr United 2 – This was far from a brilliant spectacle, the players on both sides displaying varying degrees of lethargy. The purpose in playing the match was to raise funds for Kilmarnock Infirmary. Wet weather depleted the turnout and, therefore, the takings. The season closed with a match played for the purpose of raising funds for war charities. It was Renfrewshire versus Ayrshire at Cappielow Park. In effect it was a Morton-St. Mirren select against an Ayr United-Kilmarnock select.

The Ayrshire team was: Blair (Kilmarnock), Bell (Ayr United), Hamilton (Kilmarnock), Hay (Ayr United), J. Goldie (Kilmarnock), McLaughlan (Ayr United), G. Goldie (Kilmarnock), Crosbie (Ayr United), McKenzie (Ayr United), Jackson (Ayr United) and Ingram (Ayr United). In a future age the composition of such a team would give rise to what is known as 'bragging rights'. However the argument is weakened by the fact that the team containing seven Ayr United players lost 3-0.

The absolute finale to season 1915/16 was the mournful news that Gunner George Alfred Fisher of the Royal Field Artillery had been killed. Less formally he had been known as 'Fred'. His enthusiasm for Ayr United led him to travel all over the country in support of the team and, in the season just finished, his cheery presence at Somerset Park had been missed. It would be remiss to omit mention of those who were returning home having made a partial rather than a total sacrifice. So many came back missing a limb that a charity initiative was set up under the title of The Limbless Soldiers Fund.

The greatest naval engagement of the war was the battle of Jutland which took place on 31st May, 1916. There was a variance in the reported number of British sailors killed but weighing up the conflicting numbers would still suggest that the total was in the region of 6,000. Men from Ayr were included in the fatalities. The strategic importance of seafaring activity was highlighted when the Admiralty issued an order that became law on 5th July. It restricted sketching and photography in the south-west of Scotland coastguard area between the Crinan Canal and Annan on the Solway Firth, including the Clyde estuary lochs and river. Sketching and photography were recreational pursuits beyond the domain of the average member of the population. And life on the west coast of Scotland was markedly safer than that on the east coast of England where Zeppelin attacks were raining death and destruction on civilians.

Lord Kitchener, the iconic recruitment figure of the Great War, was now dead. He was the face of the 'Your Country Needs You' poster. He drowned on 5th June, 1916, while en route to Russia on an important military mission. The ship struck a mine off the Orkney Islands but the poster bearing his image is immortal. Of course with conscription in full flow recruitment campaigns were rendered redundant.

"The hour was 7.30 a.m. and the day was Saturday, 1st July. The hour and the day will be long remembered, for it was then that the Allies, over a long section of their line in the west, began the foremost movement for which the world had waited so long." This was how the *Ayrshire Post* described the first day of the Battle of the Somme. Readers were then told that: "Never in the history of the world has such a rain of shells been poured out on an enemy." So why did this great offensive result in more than 60,000 British troops being killed, wounded or missing on that first day, the dead numbering approximately 20,000 of that total? Well, without wishing to stand accused of writing revisionist history, the conclusion can easily be drawn that the tactics were greatly inept. Tactics? Let us revise this notion and commute it to the singular. The tactic was for a line of British soldiers to walk towards the German trenches, get cut down by machine guns, then the next line would follow, step over the bodies of their comrades, get slaughtered themselves and for this process to continue. Your writer admits to being ill-qualified to comment upon military history rather than football history. Yet these conclusions are printed here after carefully researching numerous contemporary accounts, an exercise that has left no scope for dubiety. The Battle of the Somme raged on until November. What now for the future of Scottish football? There could be no case left for continuance. This argument was lost on the game's administrators.

On the evening of 21st July, 1916, the monthly meeting of the

Scottish Football League committee was held. The main item of discussion was an intimation that the Football League and the Southern League were agreeable to the continuance of the arrangement allowing their registered players to turn out for Scottish League clubs in areas where they were stationed or temporarily resident. With the non-availability of players threatening to be a certain problem rather than a probability this was a tidy arrangement. The prospective composition of the Ayr United team was indistinct. Goalkeeper Gordon Kerr was expected to be unavailable from the outset but this expectancy was wayward. In conversation John Bell had let it slip to a journalist that he was getting a job in Africa. That did not materialise and he too was able to play when the season got underway. The speculation about the other full-back, Willie McStay, was accurate and he was recalled by Celtic after having been on loan to Ayr United since November 1912. It was thought that the previous season's half-back line of Jimmy Hay, Willie Cringan and Switcher McLaughlan would at least remain intact for the time being. Four of the forwards were considered to be certain starters. They were Cammie Ingram, Alex McKenzie, Robert Cringan and John Jackson. Conspicuously absent from that list of forwards is the name of Jimmy Richardson, the ace goalscorer. Again the speculation was well founded. Bearing the title of Corporal James Richardson he was sent to fight in France and he was to make just one appearance for the club over the course of the next two seasons. Early on in his time in France he won a 15-franc prize for putting the shot. It paled in the overall scale of his achievement. This was a man who had won the Football League championship with Sunderland in 1912/13 and had been a runner-up in the same season's F.A.Cup final. Inside-forward John Jackson could have been relied upon to achieve a goalscoring consistency in the absence of Richardson but he too departed. He moved to Clyde, one of his former clubs. The intentions of outside-left Alec Gray remained unclear.

On the Saturday prior to the initial round of league engagements, Ayr United lost 3-1 to Rangers at Beresford Park. The purpose of the match was to raise funds for the Red Cross Society. Two football grounds at the disposal of the club did not quell speculation about a permanent move to Dam Park. The basis of these rumours was the fact that the lease of Somerset Park was due to expire that November. It narrowed down to the advisability of negotiating with neighbours W. G. Walker's to extend the lease of Somerset Park or whether it would be preferable to enter talks with the Ayrshire Agricultural Association for the lease of Dam Park. The notion of decamping there was not too fanciful. In February 1914 it had been reported that the directors were in negotiation over obtaining a lengthy lease. The advantages were abundant. It was a central location, the playing pitch was large and in good order and it was thought that it could be made to accommodate 50,000 at a relatively minimal cost. Again in 1916 it was fated not to materialise. Ever persistent, a further attempt was made in June 1919 on the expiry of Ayr Cricket Club's lease. The Ayrshire Agricultural Association dealt with the rival claims at that time by staging a vote amongst themselves. Ayr Cricket Club won by a substantial majority. There could have been one disadvantage to the move. The close proximity to the hospital may have meant that the noise would have disturbed patients. Interestingly when Ayr United played two League Cup ties at Dam Park in 1972, patients could be seen watching the action from the windows. St. Mirren were beaten 2-1 and Clydebank were thrashed 5-0 so, just maybe, it aided their recovery! Back in 1916 staying at Somerset Park would have found favour from the people of Newton and Wallacetown.

The news from France was horrifying. In description of trench fighting in the Great War the greatest cliché has always been the word 'attrition'. It is a virtual guarantee that this word will recur in accounts whether contemporary or not. Yet the word 'attrition' is relevant rather than being a tired old phrase used out of laziness. Battle plans, no matter how detailed, did not negate the simple truth that each side was trying to wear the other down. Mounting numbers of dead and wounded on both sides with no end in sight was the outcome. In the *Ayrshire Post, Ayr Advertiser* and the *Ayr Observer*, the obituaries of young men continued unabated. The obituary reproduced here was not untypical.

Private Andrew Duff

Mr and Mrs Duff, 21 High Street, Ayr, have been officially notified that their second son, Pte. Andrew Duff, Argyll and Sutherland Highlanders, was killed in action on the 20th July (1916). Pte. Duff, who was twenty-eight years of age, enlisted in February, 1915, and was drafted to France on 20th April this year. He leaves four children, the eldest of whom is six. The little ones are now fatherless and motherless, their mother having died about a year ago.

Under the captaincy of John Bell, Ayr United hosted Third Lanark in the opening league fixture of season 1916/17. After losing 1-0 the supporters were left to bemoan a lack of weight in the forward line. The attendance topped 4,000, many of whom would have been of military age but working in protected occupations. There were assumptions, most often wrong, that those men still at home were shirking their military duty. A 'press gang' mentality evolved whereby large batches of young men were seized by the military authorities, escorted through the streets as if they were criminals and taken to the police station to the sound of crowds shouting abuse at them. This type of activity was promiscuous and unwarranted. National statistics showed that, on average, only one man in sixty-five was detained in this way. In one extreme case there was documentary evidence of 150 being rounded up, not one of whom was detained. We can all be most grateful that we were not around in 1916. By comparison the recession-hit Britain of the modern age is a positive Utopia.

"When is all this going to end?" was the big question. There were optimists who believed that it would be over before the onset of winter. Those who thought that it would still be going on by that time the next year were defined as pessimists. By courtesy of that wonderful gift of hindsight it can be recorded here that the war was still going on *two* years later. Although there was variance in the forecasts as to the probable duration, there was more agreement as to what would bring it to an end. There was a popular belief that conditions in Germany were intolerable to the extent that chronic hunger prevailed and that unless this was alleviated it would give way to starvation. The 'submission by starvation' theory gave hope to the people of Britain.

Amidst the chaos the priority of the Ayr United team selection for Firhill was miniscule. The team selection in itself was not especially problematic. Alec Gray's non-arrival by kick-off time was the area of concern. It was reminiscent of the day in January 1915 when the squad turned up at the same venue without a goalkeeper. 'Send for Sprigger' was the 1915 solution but this time it was necessary to begin the match a man short. Gray being an outside-left, the forward line was shorn to just four players. He appeared twenty-three minutes into the contest, just after Partick Thistle had taken the lead. The final scale of defeat was 3-0 and Gray's lateness had been caused by train delays. In 1916 this was a valid reason, rather than an excuse. Troop movements and cargoes of munitions just had to gain precedence.

A week later Ayr United began with ten men again. The absentee this time was goalkeeper Gordon Kerr. With his unit being stationed in Aberdeen the finger of blame could not have been pointed. But it *was* pointed – pointed at the directors.

"The Ayr United directors have been saddled with the blame for the loss of the points and the match by turning out a team minus a man for a most vital position. Against Celtic it was doubly unwise."

On the occasion of Celtic's previous visit to Ayr, a problem had been created when it was discovered that George Getgood had left the district. The player was at fault through not giving ample notice. Gordon Kerr's non-appearance was down to nothing more than the vagaries of the time. In the obvious hope that he would turn up late, the home team started the match a man short and with John Bell deputising as a goalkeeper. Joe O'Kane scored for Celtic after just three minutes. O'Kane's success was partly due to the space created by the absence of Bell at right-back. Gambling that Kerr would not arrive, Billy Middleton, a winger, was sent on to replace John Bell in goal. Bell was then able to settle in his true position while Middleton completed the match by keeping a clean goal. The stand-in was a standout and a 1-0 defeat against formidable opponents was not without merit. Wounded soldiers watched the match from seats arranged on the track in front of the stand. They had suffered what was known as a 'blighty wound'. This was the type of wound considered bad enough for them to be sent home. Other wounds were treated in a field hospital, prior to the patched-up Tommie being sent back to the trenches to live with the fear of death again.

It is hard to conceive of 1916 having the capacity to be any worse. To that end people strove hard to make the best of an increasingly fraught existence. At a meeting of the Ayr Presbytery the Rev. Mr Duncan made a strong protest against ice cream shops opening on a Sunday. It stretches belief that this was worthy of discussion in this of all years. The lobby for observance of the Sabbath was vocal but people were really hard-pressed and they deserved to be able to avail themselves of whatever small diversions were there. The prohibition lobby was even stronger but at least the argument for a total ban on alcohol was supported by the prospective impairment of vital work. Cinemas were very popular. In September Green's Picturedrome (it still stands in Boswell Park) advertised a forthcoming film entitled *The Somme*.

George Waddell - He gave sterling war time service to Ayr United after ignoring Kilmarnock's enquiry.

The showings were scheduled to begin on 9th October. It was an extraordinary release date when it is considered that the battle was still in process and was fated to grind on until 13th November. So was there also a case for football presenting itself as a useful means of escape? It has to be said that this was still difficult to reconcile. Availability and travelling were two very large obstacles.

Ayr United were spared the handicap of starting with ten men in three consecutive games. At Kilmarnock there was a full complement from beginning to end and they all played in their conventional positions. George Waddell's inclusion at right-half for Ayr was irksome to the home club. This was his second match after joining on loan from Bradford City. Kilmarnock's enquiry for Waddell did not even get the courtesy of a reply. Relieved of goalkeeping duties, Billy Middleton scored twice in a 2-1 victory. On a later page you will be able to read precisely why he would never again appear as a goalkeeper.

"Time was when a visit from Hearts would have occasioned a great stir in Ayr but the war has made great changes."

Beating Hearts 2-0 seemed like nothing more than a matter of routine against a club that had felt the ravages of war so badly. A perfect illustration of their plight was fielding a team containing two junior players. Getting a team onto the field was a common difficulty. For their home match against Ayr, Raith Rovers were missing Welsh due to a bereavement and Palmer, who was yet another to miss a rail connection. The 3-1 Ayr win was appreciated by "the small band of Ayrshire sodgers." These men belonged to the Royal Scots Fusiliers and were stationed "somewhere on the east coast."

If ever there was proof that football can transcend anything, it came in September 1916. News of continual slaughter mixed with the day to day privations of life should have been a potent enough brew to curb the tendencies of football hooligans. It was not so. The Ayr United board felt compelled to issue this statement.

"Unless the unruly conduct of the spectators at Somerset Park during the progress of a match is discontinued it will be necessary for the management to issue instructions to refuse admission to certain individuals who are responsible for this conduct."

The tone, and to a certain degree the content, was not dissimilar to a statement issued by the board in November 2011.

"The behaviour of some Ayr United fans lately has gone beyond the acceptable legal parameters. Inside football grounds in Scotland alcohol consumption, the possession and lighting of flares and the throwing of objects which may cause injury or offence either onto the track, pitch or otherwise is prohibited. We have had a couple of meetings with some supporters' organisations to highlight the reasonable limits of behaviour and emphasising the increased financial cost to the club as a consequence of continued disregard of the ground regulations. Unfortunately, since the meetings took place, further incidents occurred at St. Mirren and at Somerset Park. A number of fans have been served with banning orders from the police and from the club itself. These were not served lightly and were only issued after receiving evidence of unwelcome or illegal behaviour."

This is not the entire 2011 statement, though enough has been culled from it to clarify the message. Clarify? Clarification is hardly needed. The combined effect of both statements screams out that the indiscipline of supporters has been genetic. It did not even originate in 1916. The first report of crowd disorder at Somerset Park dates back to 1890.

In Ayr United's seventh league fixture of the season, the team began with ten men for the third time. This time the missing player was John Bell. With the game in progress a player called "Smith" went on to fill Bell's right-back position. His identity was concealed more easily than his standard of fitness was. He was injured (or 'lame' in the terminology of the time) from the moment he went on. A 1-0 win was not especially creditable since the Aberdeen team at Ayr had been weakened by military and naval reasons.

The onset of winter necessitated earlier kick-off times in the pre-floodlighting age. These earlier starts were incompatible with clocking-off times for some places of work, now that there were extra demands. Clocking-off times? In the vernacular of 1916 clocking-off time was known as lousin' time. A modest crowd of around 3,000 for a home match with Dumbarton was easily explained as was the standard of football in the following piece of social commentary.

"It is not surprising if occasionally the football is not as good as it was in the time before the war, when the men were not so 'hard ca'ed' at work as they are now."

At 3-1 to Ayr we must surmise that the Dumbarton players were even 'harder ca-ed'.

To this point of the season Gordon Kerr's availability had been greater than anticipated. He did not get leave to play against league leaders Morton at Greenock, though with due warning Sprigger White was able to fill the void in a 2-0 defeat. The perennial problem of availability and, by association, team selection, was problematical but there was a sense of balance in the knowledge that Ayr United's adversaries often carried an equal or even greater burden. For example centre-forward Jimmy Marshall was unable to appear for a home fixture against Hibs a week later (coincidentally Ayr United had an identically named forward at the time of the outbreak of the next war). Alex McKenzie replaced Marshall but only briefly. He retired with injury so early that the team had to play for eighty-two minutes with ten men. Hibs' problems were so acute that their team had to be picked close to kick-off time because of the doubt about which players would appear. In normal times the team would have been agreed upon at a board meeting then published in the Friday newspapers. After a 2-1 home win one report was headed U10 Defeat Invaders. This was a subtle reference to the ten men winning and a less subtle analogy involving a U-10 which happened to be a class of submarine used by the Germans. It was a contest that marked the end of Billy Middleton's season. He departed with the Ayrshire Yeomanry for "somewhere at the seat of war." That 'somewhere' was France. His popularity was evidenced in the following expression. "We all sincerely hope he'll return safe to the Auld Toon when the European turmoil has quietened down." In December 1916 any quietening down of the war would owe itself to the adverse weather and nothing else. The position was one of stalemate.

With Christmas approaching Santa Claus took up residence locally in Hourstons. In something of a pre-emptive strike, the store distanced itself from any beliefs that Santa Claus was German in origin. They paid for advertisements in which an explanation was given to disprove any German links. Such was the local (and national) sensitivity to anything German. It is a reasonable assumption that anyone contracting German measles would have had it diagnosed under the alternative name of rubella.

With an assuredly cheerless Christmas still a little over a fortnight away, the chaos in the matter of picking the Ayr United team showed no signs of receding. The prospect of playing at Celtic Park would have been daunting enough at the best of times. John Bell was confined to bed with flu, so the war could not be blamed for that. Cammie Ingram, an outside-right, took Bell's place at right-back. Charlie Phillips, once of West Ham United and a veteran of the first Ayr United team in 1910, filled the outside-right position even although he was a Clydebank player. With Billy Middleton off the scene, the outside-left position was taken up by "a player named Shankly of the Glenbuck Cherrypickers." How ironic that the reference to Shankly was couched with a hint of obscurity. This was Alex Shankly, born in 1893. He was the elder brother of the eventually illustrious Bill Shankly, born in 1913, and Bob Shankly, born in 1910. In Johnny Crosbie he had a fellow Glenbuck native as a team mate on his senior debut. The line-up brought forth a comment that "Ayr

United were practically a beaten team before they entered the arena." It was an incisive observation. Time was called on a 5-0 defeat.

"It's a lang lane that has nae turnin' and the bend in the one in which Kilmarnock and Ayr United teams have been travelling since September 13th, 1913, was reached on Saturday."

On 16th December, 1916, Kilmarnock recorded their first ever league win against Ayr United in what was the eighth match in the series. Prior to that date they had not even succeeded in scoring a league goal versus Ayr United at Somerset Park. On reaching the turning point mentioned in the quote they won 2-0. The result was not dwelt upon. That would have been a discourtesy to club director and S.F.A. treasurer Tom Steen who had a function held in his honour that night. The venue was the Ayr Arms Hotel and he was presented with a silver tea service and tray, part of which bore the inscription: "Presented to Mr Thomas Steen by the directors, players and shareholders of the Ayr United Football Club Ltd., on the occasion of his marriage, 11th October, 1916." In his capacity as team captain, John Bell made a speech in which he stated a case for the club having a roll of honour for the players who had fallen in combat. He said that the idea had struck him just the previous night and that the players would be glad to subscribe towards it. Mr Gray, the chairman, gave an assurance that it would be discussed at the next board meeting. With no end of the hostilities in sight it was far from probable that the list of players killed was complete.

In today's society there is a phrase which tends to get an airing when it is deemed that someone is talking about an irrelevance. The phrase is: "What has that got to do with the price of sugar?" Around Christmastime 1916 Sir William Beale, the M.P. for South Ayrshire, commented: "The charging of sixpence per pound for sugar is causing irritation and dissatisfaction." Submarines continued their destruction of Britain's merchant shipping and there were forecasts of impending shortages of meat. Compounding the misery was the expectancy of a heavy increase in rail fares. Increased travelling costs threatened an additional financial burden on Ayr United and the club's supporters although this was a minor overall consideration.

After beating Hearts 2-1 at Tynecastle Park on 23rd December, 1916, victory was not tasted again until 10th March, 1917. Between those dates three points were taken from a possible twenty-four. Ayr United's capacity to lighten the wartime gloom was even losing momentum. The *Ayrshire Post*'s summary of the year was written in a tone that was becoming habitual.

"To call this the festive season, in this particular year of grace, would, to say the least of it, be an abuse of language. The war has dropped its heavy pall over everything. Twelve months ago we were buoyed up with the hope that lent itself so easily to expectation that the early summer would bring with it a mighty change over the scene. It did nothing of the sort. The autumn did something to restore the flickering anticipations but more recent events in eastern Europe have helped to demonstrate that the progress of the Allies has not been in the right direction. And the prospect even now is not alluring. There is no room for questioning we shall suffer less than the enemy. The only worthy attitude to take is one of hopeful assurance that we shall win through triumphantly in the end."

This message was far from teeming with hope, most especially with the opinion that "the prospect even now is not alluring." Happy New Year? When 1916 gave way to 1917 it was a hollow greeting. The *Ayr Advertiser*'s year end summary was similarly-themed.

"The year 1916, like its predecessor, closed with the grim shadow of war overhanging Europe, and during its course it brought suffering and hardship, anxiety, sorrow and grief to countless homes in many countries."

The process of selecting the Ayr United team was soon to escalate from difficult to chronically difficult. In relation to a fixture at Aberdeen on 6th January, the club intimated to the Scottish League that it would not be possible to raise a team at all. In response, permission was given to borrow players from any clubs. Conveniently, goalkeeper Gordon Kerr was stationed in Aberdeen. Rather it would have been convenient had it not been for a hurried run south with his regiment. The goalkeeping position apart, it transpired that the Ayr team was at full strength. Even at that Sprigger White was experienced enough to guard the Ayr United goal. In talking about strength, the context here is personnel. Physical strength was quite a different matter. The match was lost 1-0 and the analysis suggested that fitness levels had been left wanting. Being cooped up in a train for over four hours that morning was not conducive to good preparation. Neither was the increased workload on all or most players during the week. One reporter even ventured to suggest that: "The decadence dates from the time that Billy Middleton had to leave."

People were clinging to the hope of a big push on the Western Front. Ideally it would be a push big enough to annihilate the enemy and end the war. That hope was being frustrated by a seeming lack of action. People at home were at a loss to comprehend what our armies were waiting for. The delay was simply down to the weather conditions. One particularly romanticised outlook came close to stating that victory was near.

"Our brave troops have taken the measure of the Huns. They feel in every fibre of them that they can, and will, walk through them whenever the word is given to advance. Germany would do well to swallow their disappointment and negotiate without the loss of a single moment, for the Somme and Verdun affairs will be mild to the crumpling up which will be the fate of the German armies on the Western Front when the word is given for our troops to go. I question very much if it will be necessary for our troops to advance at all, unless the Germans try to escape by flight, then they will have to be followed and destroyed."

Walk through them whenever the word is given! By the second sentence the whole spiel had lost credibility. War was proving to have a debilitating effect on British society. A paltry attendance of around 2,000 watched Motherwell win 2-1 at Ayr. The most obvious conclusion was that people were otherwise engaged in military service or war work. Indifference induced by a combination of foundering results and war weariness may also have taken its toll.

With gate receipts deteriorating, a match at Dundee was ill-timed. The threatened sharp increase in rail fares had already been implemented as the club well knew after the experience of the previous away fixture, which had been at Aberdeen. Chartered trains for supporters would assuredly be deferred to a future day when sanity would once more prevail in the world. A normal world would not have required the passing of the Output of Beer (Restriction) Act. Pub opening hours were already restricted and now beer output was to be reduced by 30%. The driving force behind this move did not originate in morality nor the potential for an adverse impact on war production. It lay in the need to channel the ingredients of beer towards food production. Interestingly, within a matter of weeks, a report entitled Lunacy In Ayrshire mentioned alcohol as a contributory factor.

Jimmy Hay worked in a protected trade but was nonetheless consigned to the Royal Artillery. This is the campaign medal of Gunner Hay.

Protected trades, and the consequent exemption from military service, at least permitted enough spectators at

Somerset Park as could keep the club functioning. The fact that takings were depleted amounted to a grievance that the club had little control over and just had to accept. This issue was to become aggravated. Within Ayr United's catchment area were numerous mining communities. Coal mining was just about the most obvious of protected trades but that was about to change. A reduction in the export of coal and the urgent need for more troops, coerced the Government into thinking that a certain number of men should be released from the mines in order to undergo military service. In the press a statement appeared that all miners of military age would be required to present themselves for a medical examination. It was premature and a little alarmist. The notice took no cognisance of the exemptions to be granted. For instance there were exemptions for men who had entered the mining industry after 14th August, 1915, having previously been engaged in other occupations. Yet for so many others there was no escaping the call-up. For example unskilled men working on the surface had positively no chance of avoiding military service, other than through age and medical fitness.

Private Tom Clifford of the Royal Scots Fusiliers was killed by a shell on the Western Front on 19th January, 1917. He was a native of Rankinston who left behind a widow and four children. On 4th September, 1897, he had played for Ayr FC in the first league match ever contested at Somerset Park. It was a Second Division fixture against the Govan-based Linthouse. Clifford sent in the cross from which Somerset Park's first league goal was scored by Dowdles. He went on to play for Glossop, Celtic, Luton Town, Nottingham Forest and Motherwell. Tall and well built, he had the makings of a good soldier. His death came at the age of forty-two. It was an advanced age to be serving.

With Ayr United's last win becoming an increasingly distant memory, the level of stamina continued to be questioned. Even in 1917 there was an awareness of the link between fitness and diet. With food shortages threatening to become critical it was going to become harder to maintain that link. Lord Devonport became the Government minister responsible for food control. He drew up a plan outlining a voluntary system of rationing. He identified bread, meat and sugar as being the three most important staples of daily consumption. Curtailing the nation's food consumption was something he avowed to be an urgent necessity so he concocted this plan. The average weekly consumption, per person, in respect of the main commodities should be: Bread – four pounds; Meat – two and a half pounds; Sugar – three-quarters of a pound. Worsening the situation was the fact that bakers were going to be allowed to supplement their flour with oats, barley, maize or rice. To put it another way, white bread would become specky bread. And it could not be sold unless it was at least twelve hours old. Moreover it had to be in the shape of a one-piece oven-bottom loaf, or a tin loaf or a roll.

Rationing food was no more than a recommendation yet. In a pompous tone the people were told: "The nation is placed upon its honour to observe these conditions." Due recognition had to be accorded to the plight of lower income families who had proportionately higher bread consumption and for whom meat would have comprised a meagre part of their diet, even in times of peace. It was estimated that 1,000,000 tons of these foods would be saved per annum provided that the public complied.

"In these days of war with weakened teams, dearer train fares and dampened enthusiasm, the trippers will be comparatively few." No great mystical powers were required to predict that Ayr United supporters would not be descending on Ibrox Park in appreciable numbers. The crowd numbered about 12,000, almost exclusively of a Rangers persuasion, and this was actually considered to be a decent attendance. Jimmy Hay, the Ayr United captain, got barracked relentlessly for the perceived misdemeanour of being a former captain of Celtic. By the narrowest of margins (1-0) it was consecutive league defeat number six.

At a monthly meeting of the Scottish Football League a topic for discussion was whether to allow players registered under the Scottish Junior Football Association to appear at senior level in situations where it was convenient to where they lived or were stationed. It was not deemed to be necessary due to the Scottish Football Association's action in letting senior players of other clubs appear for clubs in their area. It was further noted that later kick-off times now helped players to get to matches on time.

"The team's decadence dates from about the time Billy Middleton went abroad on active service." This mournfully summed up a defeat at Dumbarton. Highly rated though he was as a winger, Middleton's career achievements would not match those of the winger who was to guest for Ayr United a week after the fall at Dumbarton.

That player was Alec Troup of Dundee. After signing for Dundee from Forfar Athletic, his debut for them had been at home to Ayr United on the opening league Saturday of 1915/16. By March 1917 he was stationed with the Royal Engineers in Largs. The club availed itself of the Scottish Football Association's blanket permission to field players stationed in the vicinity. Ironically he made his debut at home to Morton, a club located even nearer to Largs. Troupie had a great career beckoning. It was to include five Scotland appearances and a Football League title with Everton in 1927/28. Dixie Dean's sixty league goals for Everton that season created a Football League record since unbeaten. The previous record was fifty-nine and it had been created the season before by George Camsell of Middlesbrough. With time running out in the last game and Dean equalling Camsell's record, Everton got a corner-kick (at home to Arsenal). Alec Troup took it and from that cross Dean headed the ball into the net and into the record books. Jerry Kelly, also ex-Ayr United, was in the Everton half-back line that day. The legendary Dean's Everton debut had been away to Arsenal on 21st March, 1925, and his captain that day was Neil McBain, the former Ayr

Neil McBain had distinguished service in the Great War then went on to become an outstanding Ayr United player and, eventually, manager.

United great and future manager. Troup and McBain were to become team mates at Everton but they never lined up in the same Ayr United team because Neilly, although registered with the club, was away doing his bit for King and country. He represented the Submarine Service and the Black Watch. Troup's availability for Ayr United was patchy. He played in four league matches and one friendly.

On 10th March, 1917, Ayr United won 2-1 at Falkirk. It was the first win since the Saturday before Christmas. The run had comprised twelve winless league fixtures. On the next Saturday St. Mirren were beaten 2-1 for the first home league win since 25th November. Beating St. Mirren should have been of comparatively futile importance when weighed against the German retreat in France. Should have been! Yet we already know that the threat to ban supporters highlighted a fanaticism that had the capacity to indulge in tunnel vision no matter the international situation.

This mention of the international situation links conveniently to the decision of the United States to declare war on Germany on 6th April. Germany's submarine warfare had been so prolific as to ignore America's neutrality. With the promise of increased resources and manpower on the side of the Allies there was now genuine hope that the fighting could be brought to a conclusion.

"The comparatively small turnout of spectators demonstrated that the public enthusiasm for football is about exhausted in Ayr at least. The decadence of the Ayr United team in the second half of the season is responsible for the lack of interest taken in the game during that period and the cessation is not unwelcome."

This summary of the season's final league match had a depressing air to it, notwithstanding the fact that the game was actually won. Gordon Kerr, Jack Nevin, Billy Middleton and Jimmy Richardson were outstanding players who had been sorely missed but for this visit of Raith Rovers yet more war-related frustrations were visited upon the club. Alec Troup was ruled out of selection due to having been

George Nisbet - His fearlessness in the Ayr United goal would indicate that he was an asset in the trenches.

inoculated. Jimmy Marshall's withdrawal was caused by the news that his brother had been killed. The problem of picking a team was not one-sided. Raith Rovers turned up without a goalkeeper and Ayr United's back-up goalkeeper, Sprigger White, played for them while the regular George Nisbet guarded the Ayr goal. After winning 2-1 the club finished in fifteenth place in the 20-club league. This was a substantial drop from fourth a year earlier and it was going to become far worse.

At the annual general meeting a loss of £170 : 4s : 5d was announced for the year. In his address chairman Charles Gray was brilliant in his outline of the problems faced. Note his sly dig at the clubs who had not had as many players enlist.

"I hope you will, in view of the unprecedented times we are living in, consider it as satisfactory as we might expect. In dealing with a company such as ours, the two most important factors are – first, the result of the season from a playing point of view; second, the financial aspect. Your directors deeply regret the lowly league position we now occupy in the league table; to drop from fourth place to fifteenth is not one that can be considered progression and leaves no room for self congratulation. But there are certain extenuating circumstances. We find ourselves in good company in close proximity to Hearts and Queen's Park – two clubs whose ranks have been depleted to an abnormal extent in comparison with others occupying leading positions. These clubs have given unsparingly of their best to fight for King and country. We take a certain pride in our record in that thirteen of our players have joined H.M. forces and we deeply deplore four of these have paid the supreme price for devotion to their country. According to the transfer valuation of our players and taking this as the basis of their value to us, those who have joined up, and particularly those whose services we have not been able to utilise at all last season, represent to a greater degree the loss we have sustained than the number indicates. It is very apparent that, while on so many occasions our team played delightful football, we lacked the guiding spirit or master hand to bring the good work to a successful issue. Of illness and accident we have had our full share and when I say that since the advent of 1917 no fewer than nine games have resulted in our defeat by the loss of the odd goal, I think you will agree that bad luck has dogged our footsteps. I regret that on this – my first year as chairman – I should have to report a position that is somewhat unsatisfactory. Our income is considerably reduced owing to thousands of our supporters being joined up for service. We have very large munition or other national factories in which large bodies of men are employed, such as is the case in many towns in close proximity to us, and our home gates of necessity must suffer. In two games – those at Aberdeen and Dundee – due to increased railway fares and to the large expense in conveying our players to their homes in good time for work, the result was a net loss to us of £50. Despite all, I do not think there is any cause for pessimism. By providing a means of pleasant recreation for those who are exempt from military service and by entertaining – as we have done – many hundreds of convalescent soldiers residing in our midst, we have had some means of justification for carrying on this sport in such serious times."

The absolute final action of the season was a match against Stevenston United at Beresford Park. It was in aid of war funds. Ayr United won 4-2 with five trialists in the team. Stevenston had the assistance of two Ayr United players, White and Montgomery. By the time the match was reported Sprigger White had signed for them.

On the morning of 9th May, 1917, word reached Ayr that Billy Middleton had been wounded and was lying in a hospital in France. The wound, on his left arm, did not preclude him from writing a letter to secretary-manager Lawrence Gemson. Middleton would play for Ayr United again and he would also be wounded again as we will see later.

Billy Middleton - Wounded in action, patched up then wounded again.

The operations on the Western Front were largely give-and-take. At times there was a pattern of ground being gained then the same ground being conceded. An ominous calm had the effect of stalling the industrial-scale killing but was hardly conducive to hastening the date of the armistice. Reportedly the British guns were more numerous, our explosives were more devastating and the guns themselves were vastly better than those of the enemy. Reportedly!

By the early summer of 1917 the third anniversary of the declaration was closing in. Scottish football had survived thus far and the question of abandonment was no longer on the agenda. At the annual general meeting of the Scottish Football Association the Scottish Cup came up for discussion. The competition was still in a state of suspension and the plan was to resume in 1917/18. A resolution was adopted to: "Permit clubs which had qualified to compete for the competition in 1914/15 being included in the competition of season 1917/18, irrespective of their position in the Qualifying Cup competition of season 1917/18." Common sense prevailed and it remained in abeyance until after the war. Why was it even a consideration? The need for manpower in France was so desperate that voluntary enlistment was invited for men between the ages of forty-one and fifty. In Ayr and similar communities the sight of discharged-disabled men was all too common.

In the season ahead Ayr United would use forty-four players in competitive action and still finish up with the wooden spoon. That figure would be eclipsed in 1995/96 with forty-five and in 1997/98 with forty-six. However that level of turnover in those pre-Bosman years of long ago was strongly indicative of something being seriously amiss.

On 4th June the Brazilian Government declared that they would be revoking their neutrality and severing their diplomatic relations with Germany. Their actual declaration of war on Germany came on 26th October. The reason for the delay was a necessity to alter their constitution to allow their country to be in a state of war. Brazil in the war on the side of the Allies? This could hardly be categorised as a well-known fact. It opened up harbours to allied shipping in the South Atlantic. Their reason for engaging in the conflict was the German threat to neutral merchant shipping. When a U-boat sank one of their own merchant ships the Brazilians felt motivated into action. The mention of Brazil will never evoke memories of the Great War. Few readers will have had any inkling of their involvement. In 1917 that country was not synonymous with football in the way that it is now but at least the game was evolving there back then. That evolution was assisted by two former Ayr FC players. One of them was Jock Hamilton who, in 1907, became the first professional football coach in Brazil. The other was Archie McLean who emigrated there in 1912 and played internationally for them against Chile and Argentina. They called him Veadinho which meant Little Deer. On the grand scale of things Brazil's contribution to the Great War was so minimal as to have no bearing on quickening the date of the German surrender. Even China declared war on Germany. That was on 14th August, 1917, and their reason for doing so was also U-boat piracy towards their own shipping.

Up to the end of May 1917, the German death toll stood at 1,068,127 with another 254,101 missing presumed dead. Naturally this begged the question of whether these figures were accurate. Or maybe it begged no such question. People were keen to cling to any positive news and an interesting comparison was that, even by ignoring the 'missing presumed dead' statistic, the supposed number of actual enemy dead exceeded the population of Greater Glasgow.

Soldiers of the Newfoundland Regiment were stationed in Ayr that summer. They were well liked by the locals. Well, most of them were. We must exempt those of their number who incurred the wrath of the Fiscal by indulging in drunken disturbances. Even without Canadian help Ayr town centre had a widespread reputation for raucous behaviour but, in July, Ayr Town Council still voted against prohibition. In

Ayr Cemetery contains a beautiful commemoration to the Newfoundlanders.

May 1918 an article appeared in the Canadian newspaper the St. John's Daily Star. It carried glowing praise about just how much the troops of the Newfoundland Regiment loved the town of Ayr. In more modern times there was a visit from Newfoundlanders to Ayr. That was on 20th April 1975 when Ayr United beat St. John's All Stars 6-0 at Somerset Park.

On the third anniversary of the war Provost Mitchell read this declaration during a commemorative service in the Auld Kirk.

"That, on this the third anniversary of a righteous war, this meeting of the citizens of Ayr records its inflexible determination to continue to a victorious end to the struggle in maintenance of those ideals of liberty and justice which are the common and sacred cause of the Allies."

Note the use of the word 'righteous'. War clearly conflicted with Christian ideals and this was a common method for churches to declare support without compromising Christian principles.

With turmoil upon turmoil the arrival of a new football season was not headline news and an opening match at home to an Ayr and District Junior select did little to stir the emotions, even in winning 7-0. Still, the true purpose was fulfilled. It was staged to raise funds for local charities. This was indicative of the pressure upon the public to keep donating. Flag Days had been getting routinely staged in Ayr High Street on Saturdays for three years. There was a plethora of worthy causes.

Expectations were low when season 1917/18 began. Those who voiced their misgivings would be fully vindicated at the season's end. Celtic away – what an opener! A 4-0 loss was in some way redeemed by a 2-0 defeat of Hamilton Accies at Ayr in game two. This was redressed by losing 2-0 at Kilmarnock in the third match.

Losing at Kilmarnock was without historical precedent with the exception of an inconsequential Ayrshire League match on 24th April, 1911. Switcher McLaughlan failing with a penalty did have historical precedent but was an extreme rarity. The Ayr support was abnormally large considering defeat was anticipated. A favourable history in the series was insufficient to compensate for the excessive demands that the war had on the club. A glimmer of light was the return of Billy Middleton to the team following his hospitalisation in France. As expressed with a hint of Scottish terminology, it was an otherwise grim day for the supporters.

"The weather controller did his best to wash out the trippers who journeyed from Ayr to Kilmarnock. When the crowd of passengers per the relief train arrived at Kilmarnock, the rain came down in a perfect deluge and every 'close-mooth' was occupied by people seeking shelter."

This was the last match of the season for George Nisbet. He had been called up for military service and his wartime service guarding the Ayr United goal was over. In 1918/19 he appeared twice whilst on leave but it was after the armistice. It can be assumed that Nisbet was an asset in the trenches if his courage as a goalkeeper was anything to go by. This was a man whose fearless nature caused him to start more matches for Ayr United than he finished. In his last match he was taken off with a head injury. That was at Alloa on 9th February, 1926. For a player who would think nothing of going head first into a clatter of boots, the end could almost have been scripted.

Herbert Lock was borrowed from Rangers to fill the void left by Nisbet. That solved an immediate problem but the position of goalkeeper would, in time, cause a lot of angst within the overall team problems.

Happy news was a rare commodity in 1917 and it had to be savoured whenever the opportunity arose. On the Saturday morning of 15th September the national newspapers reported that Jimmy Richardson had arrived from France and would be in the team to play Third Lanark at Cathkin Park that afternoon. The source was impeccable and he played in a creditable 1-1 draw in which Johnny Crosbie scored.

On the morning of the next match Richardson departed for the Western Front but the Clyde party arrived at Ayr minus two of their players thus enhancing the possibility of a home win. Clyde managed to fill one of the positions and would have competed with ten men had it not been for the gracious action of an Ayr United reserve player being pressed into action in their team. At right-half for Ayr was someone playing under the concealed identity of "Shankly" (it was not Alex Shankly). A newcomer called McNaughton was at centre-forward but none of this prevented a 3-1 defeat and an unsympathetic headline of: From Bad To Worse. A lot worse was to come.

Airman George Duncan was an Ayr United supporter who wrote home from the front:

"I have been in _____ [censored] just over fifteen months now. How swiftly time flies even here! I never once regretted throwing in my lot with the gentlemen of the Royal Flying Corps. I am with a splendid squadron - one of the best. Honours and decorations galore have come our way and I believe that we can claim as many, if not more, Hun machines than any other squadron. And so the great game is in full swing again. I see Ayr lost to Celtic and defeated the Accies from Hamilton. We get the scores here on Mondays. I wish the United good luck."

According to the records of the Imperial War Museum the life expectancy of a new pilot on the Western Front in 1917 ranged between eleven days and three weeks. George Duncan must have defied the odds and returned to Somerset Park. This is based on the fact that he was not listed amongst the war dead.

"It is with the greatest regret that we have to chronicle the fact that, as an outcome of their visit to Clydebank last Saturday, Ayr United now occupy the humiliating position of being last in the Scottish League table."

Beyond all shred of doubt the *Ayrshire Post* football writer was an unashamed supporter of the club. His reports were regularly punctuated with emotive expressions and you can feel his pain seeping through from these words. His first six words replicated the standard introduction to the communications sent to inform relatives that a loved one had died. There were valid reasons for losing at Clydebank. Jimmy Hay was unfit, Willie Cringan elected to play for Celtic on loan, Billy Middleton was compelled to play in a military match, McNaughton had got injured in his debut the week before and for reasons that were unapparent (but probably injury) Brock did not play either. In times of crisis, Celtic manager Willie Maley could be relied upon to be sympathetic to the Ayr United cause and this time he was ultra generous by lending McInally, Hyslop and Brodie. Alec Maley, his brother, was the manager of Clydebank and we might contemplate that family relations could have been strained had it not been for the home side winning 3-1.

A resumption of horse racing was a small concession to normality. A race meeting was held in Scotland for the first time since May 1915 and the venue was Ayr. The Western Meeting was attended by a large crowd in miserable weather. It would have been erroneous to interpret this as a small chink of light in those dark days. War commentators were most eloquent in putting forth views as to how a negotiated peace could be obtained but such opinions were rendered hollow when their arguments were dependent on Germany making concessions on a major scale. Money, or the lack of it, had some potential for a cessation of the fighting. In October 1917 the Chancellor of the Exchequer had to justify the cost of the war to the House of Commons. This was far from the simplest of tasks considering that it was costing the country £6,648,000 a day and there was no inkling that this would decrease. Germany's fiscal position was described as "deplorable beyond comprehension."

At 6 a.m. on 4th October, the British mounted a massive attack in Flanders. Very quickly there were reports of excellent British progress, light casualties and large batches of German prisoners being taken. We can rest safe in the knowledge that the German-based media would have had a different take on it.

Webb, a Dubliner, played poorly for Ayr United in a 1-1 draw away to St. Mirren and there were no conflicting accounts. Yet the whole horrible morass of team selection allowed him to be retained when Falkirk called at Ayr. There was little in the way of competition for places. Completing the team list was an inordinately problematical task in itself. Although he was leading the attack, the Dubliner failed to score in a 4-0 win and he was not seen in an Ayr shirt again. It was reported that George Waddell "got rid of his alias for the day", the implication being that he had been playing under an assumed name for reasons of national security. The paying public knew who he was but they couldn't let the enemy find out! Within the week Waddell and his alias had gone. The fighting in Flanders remained heavy and it was known that mobilisation was just a matter of time for some of his colleagues.

Centre-half Willie Cringan's appearances had become increasingly fleeting given his tendency to prefer playing for Celtic on loan. When Ayr United were losing 2-0 away to Hearts he was playing in an Old Firm derby (Rangers 1 Celtic 2). Armadale's Hardie became Ayr's fifth consecutive centre-half. Losing to Hearts was simply terrible with the consequence that: "Ayrshire this week occupies the two extremes in the Scottish League table." Yes, the shame of being bottom of the league was aggravated by Kilmarnock being top. How had it come to this? Well, the policy of engaging loan players may have been a cause. McStay, Waddell, Jackson, Marshall, Montgomery, Yule and Troup had all been registered with other clubs and there appeared to be no power to prevent Willie Cringan donning the hoops of Celtic. Acquiring George Nisbet from Petershill in February had been a smart piece of business but that too had been undone by the call of the Army. Reports that Jimmy Hay was "on the eve of departure" transpired to be premature. Gunner Hay was indeed fated to be immersed in the conflict but not just yet.

"The method of playing men from other clubs has now left the Somerset Park management very poorly off for talent.

If Ayr United can now locate junior players of outstanding merit we may yet see the team a good bit removed from the position they now occupy in the table. The building of the Ayr United team is now at a transitionary state and we are never certain of the composition of the team till it takes the field."

Players being called to arms was beyond the control of the club but the argument here was that by minimising loan arrangements there would be less vulnerability to other clubs having first call on them while they were still on Scottish soil.

Sugar had become so scarce that Co-operative stores issued cards to people in order to limit the quantity they were buying. Within several weeks of that initiative it was announced that wounded Tommies would no longer get their free cup of tea at Somerset Park due to the local Food Committee's refusal to give the directors the necessary permit for an allowance of sugar. Could they not have drunk tea without sugar? Positively not. In 1917 this would not have been remotely considered. It would have been spat out without hesitation. There were shortages in other staple products too. Queues were emerging in Ayr when it was known that there were stocks of butter or margarine.

Cold weather conspired with the new found bottom-of-the-league status to stunt the attendance to marginally over 2,000 for the visit of Hibs. The Ayr centre-forward had his name concealed as "Thomson". He was instantly recognisable as Alex Bennett, who had a very high profile in the Scottish game as a Rangers player who used to be with Celtic. We can only ponder why the publication of his real name would have assisted Germany's war effort! He went on to complete nine matches in the black-and-white hoops of Ayr United and he scored in none of them.

Bennett did not play against his parent club on the occasion of a 0-0 draw against Rangers at Ibrox Park. In description of goalkeeper Herbert Lock it was written that: "He had a strenuous afternoon's work." His performance was not lost on the home supporters who were quick to voice the opinion that he should still have been guarding the Rangers goal.

One point was gleaned from the next seven matches and the despair of the times was typified at Falkirk.

"The composition of the team was in doubt right up to the starting time, and when the eleven did turn out it was revealed that the directors must indeed have been in sore straits to get all the places filled."

Arriving at Brockville Park without a goalkeeper was the largest problem to address. The solution was to borrow a Falkirk player who adopted the name "Smith". Johnny Crosbie was not with the Ayr United party therefore Billy Middleton made the switch to inside-right from his customary outside-right position. Andrew Brown, an outside-left, was recalled to the first team at outside-right. Archie Somerville, a half-back, was fielded at centre-forward in the absence of Alex Bennett (or "Thomson" if we are to comply with censorship!) and for the second time so far in the season Barry was borrowed from Third Lanark to play at centre-half. It was a complete mess and the few travelling supporters expected defeat. Their expectation materialised to the extent of 3-0.

To lose 3-0 at Falkirk was one issue. Losing 3-0 at home to Kilmarnock was quite another. Trials and tribulations were being experienced by all clubs. To suggest otherwise would be churlish and inaccurate. Yet this did not alleviate the discomfort of this particular Ayrshire derby comprising bottom versus top.

The Royal Flying Corps, based at Turnberry, had a football team playing at junior level. It was announced that they would be playing their future home matches at Beresford Park on Saturdays when Ayr United were playing away. It was highly questionable whether the public had a stomach for fortnightly football far less weekly football. The estimated attendance of 3,000 for the Kilmarnock fixture was actually considered to be satisfactory.

Winter's onset was railing against attendances. Early dark had the inevitable consequence of earlier kick-off times with the further consequence of people often being unable to get away from work on time. This applied equally to players. Bell and Brock did not play against Morton because they could not get away in time to catch a suitable train to Ayr. The respective captains in the Morton match were ex-Annbank players Jimmy Hay and Jimmy Gourlay. This snippet induced less interest than the strangers in the Ayr shirts. Brewster, registered with Aberdeen, played at right-half in a 1-0 defeat as did Hennessey of Third Lanark at centre-half. George Brewster would, in the year ahead, win the Military Medal. In the post war years he went on to play for Everton and Wolves and would make a Scotland appearance. In 1917/18 he went on to make thirteen league appearances for Ayr United.

When the nets were left unspoiled in a match against Partick Thistle it comprised four consecutive home matches without an Ayr goal. This dubious record was equalled between October and December 1999. Taking all matches into account, another adverse statistic here in 1917 was one Ayr United goal over the course of seven consecutive fixtures and it scarcely mattered anyway since it was in a 5-1 rout at Motherwell. Deeper scrutiny in the matter of goalscoring analysis also revealed that when the team went to Airdrie on 22nd December, no Ayr United centre-forward had scored in any game that season with the exception of a charity match against a Junior Select.

The centre-forward drought was addressed in inglorious circumstances. The match was lost 4-1 and the marksman was a player called Neilson who was borrowed from Airdrie, the home club. On the same afternoon there was a sensational development at Celtic Park. Since joining Ayr United from Sunderland, severe doubts could have been harboured about which club held Willie Cringan's registration. His fondness for being a Celtic loanee either could not or would not be restrained. After Celtic had beaten Dumbarton 3-0 he was arrested. Then, on the Monday (Christmas Eve), he appeared in the Eastern Police Court in Glasgow on a charge of being an absentee under the Military Service Act. He appeared before the same court twice more. At the third appearance the charge was withdrawn and by May 1918 he was in the Royal Air Force. On a personal note it may be added that I lived in Bathgate as an infant and Willie Cringan lived there then. My father knew him and attended his funeral in 1958.

Christmas in 1917 was reminiscent of the one before and the one before that. The carol proclaiming "Peace on earth" could not be sung with conviction. The greeting "Goodwill to all men" rang just as hollow. A supreme irony was war being waged in the Holy Land, the British having entered Jerusalem on 11th December on driving out the Turks.

There was one item of good local news. The Freedom of Ayr was accorded to Lieutenant Robert Shankland of the Canadian Infantry. Having already won the Distinguished Conduct Medal in the summer of 1916, he had the ultimate distinction of winning the Victoria Cross for conspicuous bravery at Passchendaele on 26th October, 1917. He was born locally at Gordon Terrace on 10th October, 1887, and his first experience of military discipline was in the 2nd Ayr Company of the Boys' Brigade. In 1911 he had emigrated to Winnipeg and his parents stayed in Wallacetown at 68 Church Street. His brief return to the town saw him regaled by civic dignitaries. It was a rare boost to the townsfolk. In the present time his Victoria Cross is on display in the Canadian War Museum in Ottawa.

Five days after his first court appearance, Willie Cringan was in the Celtic team that won at Ayr. Three of the Ayr team had concealed identities. "Cameron" was described as "a famous back". There were no clues as to who "Morton" was but he did score in the 2-1 defeat. "Thomson" was Alex Bennett.

On 2nd January, 1918, Ayr United beat the Royal Flying Corps 4-2 in a friendly. Then, by taking full points in the next two fixtures (3-0 at Hamilton) and 2-1 at home to St. Mirren, the seemingly eternal propensity for bleakness diminished by virtue of moving off the bottom place. Disguising the true names of players took match reporting into the realms of farce. "Cameron", the "famous back", shared his disguise

John Cameron - His war resembled fiction.

with another who played in the same position. In relation to the team picked to play St. Mirren it was confusingly reported that: "Cameron number 1 displaced Cameron number 2 at right-back." So far as is known, the German code breakers could not fathom it!

By the early part of 1918 an awareness was creeping in that the shape of post-war Britain was a concern that required attention. Would councils have the capacity to provide houses for discharged soldiers? Such dialogue had no recourse in developments in the theatres of war. A big push to wipe out the enemy was ensconced more in hope than reality. Already eliminated was the notion of a negotiated peace settlement. It would take unconditional surrender and nothing else. In 1917 there had been political commentators who spoke about calling it a draw. This would have meant a ceasefire and the powers involved agreeing to a resumption of the pre-August 1914 position. Though interesting, it was a far-fetched theory.

On 25th January, the Ayr Local Food Committee held a meeting at which it was agreed to adopt the rationing scheme recommended for the whole country. Note the word 'recommended'. Individual councils, although having discretionary powers, were compelled to act by the prevailing conditions. In Ayr there had been unedifying scenes in which women were almost hostile in the way they had laid siege to shops that stocked rare but essential foodstuffs. This was now being addressed by the introduction of ration cards for butter, margarine and tea. The scheme followed the one already in place for sugar.

The severity of the food situation was reflected by the Board of Agriculture writing to Ayr Town Council stating that they were of the opinion that forty acres of the Old Racecourse should be ploughed up and put under the crop. Note that this was worded in a conciliatory rather than a mandatory tone. The letter was in response to an earlier threat from the Ayrshire Food Production Committee that non-compliance in the matter would lead to them recommending the Board of Agriculture to issue an order compelling it. After debating the issue, the councillors put it to a vote. The only two who were agreeable to ploughing it up were the proposer and the seconder. Its continued use for grazing was the agreement of all the others. It was a brave stand-off. The Board of Agriculture wrote back to say that they would not insist on the cultivation of the Old Racecourse. One of the town's earliest football venues therefore became preserved for recreational use. But the mere staging of this episode was strongly indicative of desperate times.

Jimmy Hay was the Ayr United captain and, in the event that he was unavailable, the role was assumed by Billy Middleton. Hay was a natural choice as captain. He had won six consecutive league titles with Celtic whom he had also captained. The captaincy of Scotland and Newcastle United had also been part of his illustrious career.

By 1918 he was a miner. Of that there was no doubt. He was working at the coalface of Drumley Colliery and had been engaged in this work since 25th July, 1915. Why then, on 22nd February, 1918, did he have to make an appearance before the Ayrshire Appeals Tribunal to answer the contention that he was eligible for military service? The agent representing him said that Jimmy had been a miner from his early youth. In response the sheriff was quick to assert: "If he is a regular miner then he should not be before us." The agent went on to clarify that the case for military exemption had been dismissed because his occupation had been a professional footballer prior to 25th July, 1915. It was clear that football was not the sheriff's forte. He had no idea that the man standing before him was a footballing legend. On asking Jimmy when he had last played football the reply was "a fortnight ago." The sheriff then quickly terminated proceedings. "Appeal dismissed" was his retort. Thus, a man who was working in a protected trade, coal mining, was deemed not to be a miner because he used to be a professional footballer. His appeal against military service was not born of a natural instinct to preserve life and limb. He was supporting a wife, four children and his elderly parents.

Jimmy Hay played at Dumbarton on the day after the tribunal hearing and at home to Motherwell a week later. Then he reported for military service with the Royal Artillery. By then the team was in the midst of a run of no wins in the last eight league games. Over the period of six consecutive Saturdays six different goalkeepers played.

Yet more drudgery was visited upon the people with the announcement that national meat rationing was coming into operation on 7th April. A far greater horror at this time was the prospect of losing the war altogether. On the Friday night of 22nd March a German advance took place on the Western Front. It exceeded fifty miles in length. It was both predicted and expected, intelligence reports having correctly conveyed news of a huge enemy troop build-up. Massive gunfire preceded an advance which even the British press admitted was overwhelming. One contemporary press report went on to describe it in these terms.

"The forces were thrown into the British fire with the most reckless prodigality of human life. The slaughter was terrible. Rank went down upon rank. Our gunners were weary with sheer slaughter. Their shot ploughed up and through the densely packed masses of the Germans. The living climbed over the dead, division after division decimated and riven. Still they advanced, and the combined weight of their infantry and artillery was so great that they broke through the British defensive system facing St. Quentin, with the result that our right wing, heroically fighting all the way, was compelled to fall back across the area devastated by the Germans in their Somme retreat and to take up new positions along the line of the Somme. All accounts testify to the heroic stand made by the British in face of the overwhelming hordes of the enemy. All day the struggle waged on wide fronts."

This account was wide open to critical analysis. It is true that there were massive German casualties but the same was true of the British. And it still amounted to a large retreat, regardless of the positives woven into such gratuitous use of poetic licence. A commonly held perception was that a big push would end the war but it had been anticipated that the push would come from our own side. In March and April 1918 there were genuine grounds for believing that Germany might win the war.

The response of the British Government reeked of panic. Military age was raised to fifty and even fifty-five for men with special qualifications. More men were to be conscripted from the mines and even munition works.

A victim of the German offensive was Billy Middleton. After being wounded in May 1917 he was patched up and sent back to fight. In April 1918 his left hand was so badly shot that his war was over. Although his Ayr United career would resume, the state of his hand would ensure no repetition of his deputy goalkeeping stint against Celtic in September 1916.

Entering the final league Saturday, Ayr United were kept off bottom place by Clyde's inferior goal average. On the assumption that Clyde were capable of beating Third Lanark at Shawfield, ignominy stood to be avoided if Hibs could be beaten at Easter Road. Jimmy Hay's military service was in the vicinity of Edinburgh and he was able to return to the team. Joe Dodds (left-back) and Andy McAtee (outside-right), both of Celtic and stationed in the area, guested in the Ayr team versus Hibs. McAtee scored in a 1-1 draw. Clyde won 2-0 to ensure that the wooden spoon was bound for Somerset Park.

A significant result the next day was the shooting-down and death of Baron von Richtofen, better known as the Red Baron. Even the Allies acknowledged that he was the world's greatest airman. This was quite a compliment considering the usual hostility to anybody or anything German and the fact that he had wrought death and destruction on the allied cause.

News reached the town that Hugh Kerr had died on 10th April, from wounds received in action. After signing from Westerlea the night before, he had made his Ayr FC debut against St.Bernard's in a Second Division fixture at Somerset Park on 15th August, 1903. It was the occasion of a 2-0 win in which he scored both goals. He took his league total to five in addition to three in the Scottish Qualifying Cup. Then, on 6th January, 1904, he was transferred to the club formerly known as Newton Heath but then in their second season as Manchester United. By the time he took up arms he was resident in the Plumstead district of south east London and therein we have the explanation as to why he joined the 14th Battalion of the London Scottish. After serving at the front for nine months he was admitted to a hospital in France on 29th March,1918, suffering from severe gunshot wounds in the right leg and left foot. Up until 7th April there were hopes of a recovery but a rapid deterioration resulted in his death, at the age of thirty-six, three days afterwards. He was buried at the Etaples Military Cemetery.

At the Ayr United annual general meeting the balance sheet showed a loss of £164 : 6s : 4d on the year's workings. William Ferguson, the club chairman, presided over a small attendance and he paid a warm tribute to Lawrence Gemson who was retiring as secretary-manager. Mr Gemson told the meeting that he wished to make it known that his resignation was wholly and solely due to health considerations and the impact of his school and other work demanding his attention in such a way as to leave him no time to fulfil the onerous duties to Ayr United. The chairman went on to explain the reasons for the operating loss and in doing so there were no surprises. So great was the turnover of players that only once had it been possible to field the same team on consecutive Saturdays. On too many Saturdays the weather had been atrocious and the impact was obvious. A total of £37 : 19s : 10d had been collected at home matches for war charities. Although not mentioned at the meeting, this represented a substantial drop in comparison to the sums being collected earlier in the war. Charity fatigue had become an affliction. The club had shown support for the troops by sending fifty footballs and a complete set of jerseys over the year.

The Scottish game had evolved into a pattern but it was an untidy one. Regulations had long since been relaxed to allow clubs to get a team onto the field regardless of which club held a player's registration. In what had become a big free-for-all there was next to no danger of clubs being fined for registration offences. When the Scottish Football Association's annual general meeting lasted no more than a few minutes it was known that season 1918/19 would conform to similar practices. The oxymoron 'organised chaos' would be a descriptive way of summarising it.

In late May 1918 the town of Ayr descended into chaos and, since it involved strike action, it actually was organised. There were four major strikes at the same time. Between forty and fifty corporation workers came out over a grievance relating to a war bonus of five shillings a week that they had been granted. The area of dispute was that they wished it to be backdated to 16th March. Employees affected were street sweepers, roads and bridges employees and cemetery workers. A visible consequence was the streets being in a mess. At Ayr Harbour 250 workers downed tools and an eerie silence descended over a scene more normally associated with the daily hubbub. Again the issue was money. At the worsted spinning mills of James Templeton and Son in Mill Street about 300 went on strike. The reason? Insufficient wages! A strike of boot and shoe operatives in Maybole caused their counterparts at the St.Crispin Works in Ayr (about 100) to come out in sympathy.

The origin of such widespread disaffection was clear. People were working harder and longer in support of the war effort and they wanted a fair reward for it. The argument may have been lost, however, on the crews of boats docking at an unproductive harbour after running the risk of being torpedoed to get there. Literally and metaphorically the town was in a mess. Renewing Ayr United season tickets lay somewhat low in the scale of priority.

These disputes caused a degree of revulsion when the natural comparison was drawn with troops risking life and limb. Patriotism, though noble, could not deflect from the fact that people were feeling the strain of the war effort both physically and mentally. The labour situation was so chronic by May 1918 that the Ministry of National Service asked schools to release boys during term time to work as agricultural labourers. Misery continued to pile upon misery. The Food Committee in Ayr agreed to an increase in the price of bread and the threat of fewer 'jeely pieces' was compounded by the threat to ration jam to one ounce per head per week. Paper supplies were running so short that newspaper readers were being urged to pre-order with their newsagent. Tram services were being cut back in the town at the behest of the Board of Trade. This was to economise in the coal needed to generate the electric power. By October schools were being asked to consider shorter days in order to preserve stocks of coal. An increasing number of soldiers returning from the front line with tuberculosis was another facet of life in Ayr in 1918. Even when the local strikes were getting resolved, the corporation workers stuck to their principles and the streets remained a mess.

"We are in the throes of what is going to prove the most critical week of the Great War." When Sir Auckland Geddes said these words in June he was alluding to the efforts to stem the German offensive. Fresh enemy divisions arriving at the Western Front served to increase the critical nature of it all. It was frightening. Germany winning the war remained a realistic possibility. The *Ayrshire Post* carried the following, probably a Press Association report, in their issue of 14th June. It was headed: THE PROSPECT OF A BLOODY SUMMER.

"There is talk of the bloodiest summer Europe has ever known. If the Germans can manage it at all, they will force an issue before the close of the season."

For anyone with enough willpower left, there was the forthcoming football season to look forward to. Or was there? A plot was afoot to get Ayr United expelled from the league.

The appointment of John Cameron as secretary-manager was a positive development. (There is an account of his career in a separate section). That was before details of the plot began to unravel. Finishing foot of the previous season's league table had no implications for relegation. The concept of automatic promotion and relegation was still in the future and, besides, the Second Division had been suspended for the duration. Subject to a guarantee being met, clubs split the gate money and there was a certain resentment that the pickings could have been better at Ayr in 1917/18. At a meeting of the Scottish Football League Committee "restricted travelling difficulties" was used as an excuse for getting rid of those clubs not matching up in terms of financial requirements. Crowds at Ayr had been alright until the demands of war had reached excessive levels and now there was a hint of a proposal that would effectively throw certain clubs to the dogs. The business was deferred until 17th July.

On the resumption of the issue it was decided to expel Ayr United and Falkirk. The travelling issue was a flimsy pretext. Having had a sniff of what might happen, the Ayr United board got a written assurance from the Glasgow and South Western Railway Company that it was "very improbable" that there would be any abolition of the 1.05 p.m. train from Glasgow to Ayr, this being a service considered most suitable for travelling teams. Falkirk's argument was even more potent since they were ideally situated, roughly halfway between Glasgow and Edinburgh. Scottish football has an extensive history of money-grabbing self interest and this was one of its earlier episodes. The gates at Ayr did not suit certain clubs, yet in the season prior to the one recently completed, the crowds had been far better than those of some of the clubs now trying to get rid of Ayr United. There were some very interesting names amongst the ten clubs who voted for this. Kilmarnock! Yes, Kilmarnock! Antipathy towards Ayr United was a more likely reason than travelling difficulties. The distance between the towns was about thirteen miles. Kilmarnock's action induced rage in the football writer of the *Ayrshire Post*.

"It'll take many a year for Ayr people, aye, and more than Ayr people, to forget such an action."

Queen's Park voting for this was nothing short of a shock. It had generally been considered that there was a special relationship with that club. Since 1914 they and Ayr United had been the sole contestants for the Ayr Charity Cup. Celtic and Rangers, traditionally driven by commercial interests, were in on the deed but Celtic comprised another club whom Ayr United were considered to have a good relationship with, principally on account of the friendship between Lawrence Gemson and Willie Maley. Partick Thistle's involvement actually bordered on the aggressive. George Easton, their delegate, told the meeting: "We will burst up the League if you don't agree." The 'we' to whom he was referring comprised fellow Glasgow clubs. Third Lanark, Hibs, Airdrie, Hamilton Accies and Dumbarton made up the remainder of the ten clubs voting to get rid of Ayr United and Falkirk. Those who voted to retain the clubs were Hearts, Aberdeen, Dundee, Raith Rovers and, of course, Ayr United and Falkirk. Pertinently Aberdeen, Dundee and Raith Rovers had taken no part in the league during season 1917/18. Motherwell, Clyde, Morton and St. Mirren abstained.

A one-year lapse on Ayr United was too severe. Director Tom Steen was still the treasurer of the Scottish Football Association and he had this to say.

"I think there is nothing for it but to close down entirely, and if we are readmitted at the close of the war we will have to begin all over again. The extraordinary thing is that if the argument about railway travelling had anything to do with it, Kilmarnock, our nearest neighbour, still voted for the exclusion of Ayr. We are to be compensated but only for unnecessary expenses. What about the goodwill of the club and players? At the present time we have £1,500 invested in players who are on active service and the club has only recently appointed a new manager."

Mr Steen may have been resigned to closing down entirely but the supporters would not concede to it. A public meeting was called, the planned venue being the Council Hall. So many people turned up that evening that an adjournment had to be made to the Town Hall. The gathering of approximately 700 was addressed by former club chairman Charles Gray who was supported on the platform by directors and officials of the club. He was at his articulate best when he made the points that the whole issue had been rushed and that insufficient consideration had been given to the financial and other interests at stake. Gathering momentum, his speech continued in these terms.

"A grave injustice has been done to the Ayr Club and to football in Ayr generally. The strenuous times in which we are living demand that the workers at home who are doing so much to support the soldiers in the field should have reasonable recreation. Lieutenant Alston of the Royal Air Force, speaking in Glasgow the other night, declared that it was the best footballers and the best sportsmen who make the best fliers. With the exception perhaps of Queen's Park and Hearts, Ayr United have sent more men than any other team in the league to H.M. Forces."

Mr Gray concluded his talk by dwelling on the serious implications of the club suspending operations, even for one year.

When the issue was thrown open to the assembled mass, the penchant for diplomacy went into sharp decline. This we know from the observation that: "In the course of subsequent discussion, strong language was employed in criticism of the decision of the League Committee." On the motion of Mr Gray it was agreed to send the following letter to the League and to the individual clubs.

"The representative meeting of members and supporters of Ayr United, protest strongly against the action of the Scottish League, in excluding the club from the League competition. We submit that no case has been made out to justify such a drastic measure at the present time. The suspension of the activities of the club is greatly detrimental to all the interests of sports in the town and neighbourhood, especially in these trying times. We therefore respectfully request the League to reconsider their decision."

There was popular support. Right from the day after the expulsion was made known, there had been a flood of comment favourable to Ayr United and Falkirk in the national media. The *Athletic News* reasoned:

"The exclusion of Falkirk and Ayr United from the forthcoming season's Scottish League tournament has met with a popular resentment that must have convinced this League that the public do not think that this body has acted either fairly or consistently."

Gladly, the weight of public opinion was strong enough and, at a special meeting of the Scottish League, the decision to exclude Ayr United and Falkirk was overturned. That was not quite the end of the matter. It left the issue of harbouring a simmering resentment of the clubs that had conspired in this whole dark deed. At board level, the relationship with Kilmarnock had been cordial because it was dictated by protocol. The local media and supporters were not similarly restrained. Grudge matches awaited. It could just about have been forgotten that there was a war on.

Terrific developments on the Western Front had forced the Germans back and they were on the defensive by early August, 1918. A headline of THE BROADENING OF THE NEW DAWN would prove to be prophetic. The gains made by the British and the French gathered pace. Later in the month a war correspondent noted: "We have had a long time to wait for the turn of the tide, and very trying, weary waiting it has been. It has taken four weary years to bring about the great change. Now it is coming. The tide has turned and it is running strong. The gains go on multiplying day by day on these old battlefields of the Somme and the Scarpe."

Whenever the Germans had been victorious in epic battles, their people at home loved to indulge in excessive celebration signified by bell-ringing. In the Britain of August 1918 the favourable war developments were marked by restraint.

People were mindful that our troops were still getting killed. A German counter offensive could have negated some of those gains but there seemed little likelihood of that happening. Anticipation of an end to it all would not have been misplaced. Politicians and commentators were beginning to speculate about peace terms. Peace terms? Let us amend that to surrender terms. Nothing short of unconditional surrender would be contemplated.

The reprieved Ayr United began the season with a metaphorical battle in a home fixture against Third Lanark. You will understand the context of this description by reference to the game's finale. John Cameron utilised his connections to sign goalkeeper John Eadon, formerly of Tottenham Hotspur. Three minutes from the end of his Ayr United debut, the team went 2-0 down when Allan scored with a header. It was a debut for Allan too, having signed from Renfrew Juniors. Just before the end Eadon dived on the ball and clutched it. When he was trying to get back onto his feet Allan kept hacking away at him in an attempt to loosen his grip on the ball. Eadon did manage to clear the ball but it did not end there. He kicked Allan and left him in great pain. Thus one debutant was ordered off and another was carried off.

Billy Middleton was re-signed in time for the next match. Wounded, patched up, sent back, wounded again – what a war! He now had his old place back in the Ayr United forward line and there was no prospect of a return to the trenches.

It was tragically ironic that the progress of the war was favourable yet the news of fatalities could not be stemmed. On 2nd September, Second Lieutenant William Kerr got killed at the age of thirty-seven while serving with the Machine Gun Corps of the 4th Battalion Royal Scots Fusiliers. He left a widow and one child in his native Beith. In his footballing days he had been a goalkeeper for Parkhouse. He was buried in the Faubourg D'amiens Cemetery at Arras. Around the same time a report emerged that Gunner Archibald Campbell had been "dangerously wounded" while serving with the Royal Field Artillery. This was a man with a special place in the history of Ayr United. Back in 1910 he had scored the club's first ever league goal and in the interim period he had played for Abercorn and Albion Rovers. On 14th September he died of his wounds at the age of thirty-eight. He left a widow and two children in Kirkintilloch and was buried at La Kreule Military Cemetery in the Flanders town of Hazebrouck.

In the context of the Second World War, Winston Churchill said the following in a speech on 9th November, 1942: "This is not the end. It is not even the beginning of the end. But it is, perhaps, the end of the beginning." There was a close historical precedent. In the context of the Great War, Bonar Law, the Chancellor of the Exchequer, had this to say on 30th September, 1918: "It is the beginning of the end."

Bonar Law was able to say this with confidence. The Hindenburg line, the Germans' supposedly impregnable line of defence, had just been breached. Towns and villages in France and Belgium were being reclaimed from the enemy and there was further good news from Palestine where the Turks were being cleared out. The victorious momentum was maintained thereby ensuring that victory was close.

When Ayr United beat Hearts 3-2 at Tynecastle Park on 12th October, the team had the backing of loud Ayrshiremen who were in their khaki uniforms. It was fast reaching the stage whereby there would be no war left for them to fight. Yet there still seemed to be little reduction in the number of obituaries appearing for our fallen troops.

Neil McBain cut an unfamiliar figure in the black and white hoops when he played in a 2-0 win at home to Queen's Park a week later. Despite signing as far back as 30th May, 1914, the total of his appearances prior to this fixture amounted to seven in the league and one in the Ayr Charity Cup. War service was, of course, the reason. From this date onwards he was now available although still awaiting discharge.

One player definitely discharged was Jimmy Richardson. After being in France for a considerable time he got shipped to England where he spent time in a hospital in order to get treatment for stomach troubles. His improvement was too slow for a return to the fighting. Instead he returned to Ayr and gradually gained strength, though an early return to football was not expected. Well, the unexpected happened and he was thrown into the fray for a home match with Hibs. What happened next was the stuff of fiction. Still not free of the scars of battle, he scored a hat-trick in a 5-0 rout.

On the Western Front another rout was coming to a conclusion. On the night of 7th November, news reached Ayr that Germany had accepted terms and that an Armistice had been signed. This news was courtesy of "a usually well informed source." Well, the pertinent word here is 'usually'. The source this time was misinformed. Just after 5 a.m. on Monday, 11th November, the Armistice was signed and it was agreed that the fighting would cease at 11 a.m. in order to allow time for the news to be communicated.

Telecommunications ensured that the town of Ayr remained abreast of what was happening and that there would be no repeat of the Boer War scenario whereby the conflict was over and the people did not know. To begin with, 11th November was a regular Monday in the town although it was tinged with an air of anticipation. On the stroke of 11 a.m. there was no change. It was as if the public awaited some manner of official gesture. If they were waiting for a sign they got it. At 11.20 a.m. the hooter at the shipyard went off with a shrill blast. Then sirens and foghorns broke out from the direction of the harbour. Public works on the Newton side of the river joined in the collective din by letting their hooters off. People needed a focal point and, in a remarkably short space of time, a crowd collected in the Sandgate, opposite the Town Hall. On hearing that a crowd had congregated there, workers at the shipyard, the harbour and other works in the vicinity, downed tools and headed to join the throng. One youngster was bold enough to breach the entrance of the building whereupon he started to get the bell tolling before an

Jimmy Richardson - Still not recovered from a stomach wound suffered in trench warfare, he returned to score a glorious hat-trick.

official sanction had been given. The Town Council had just concluded their first sitting after being reconstituted when they got word of the assembled mass outside. They adjourned to the Committee Room which had windows overlooking the Sandgate. From one of those windows Provost Mathie-Morton addressed the crowd in what was his first public appearance since his appointment.

"Fellow citizens, this is a glorious day. For over four years we have been tortured by this grievous war. Calls have been made again on our young men, who have gone forth like martyrs to save us. For four years they have endured the tortures and the miseries of the battlefield, and they have carried our banners far and near to victory."

Thus began a speech punctuated by cheering. It must have been an emotional address considering his youngest son had been killed in battle in May 1915.

The bell-ringing was predictable as was the display of flags from windows all over the town. These flags appeared with such rapidity as to imply that the people must have had them ready in anticipation of this day. Children yelled themselves hoarse as they ran about waving miniature Union Jacks. Bunting and flags got hoisted on public buildings. All of the tramway cars were decorated and the same treatment was afforded to horse and motor vehicles. Crowds paraded the streets and the people were greatly animated throughout the day. The band of the Royal Scots Fusiliers emerged from the barracks and marched through the town playing patriotic airs.

The peace celebrations at the conclusion of the Boer War had been marred by riotous scenes fuelled by alcohol. That just had to be on the minds of the magistrates when the suggestion was made to close the town's pubs at one o'clock. Some did not open at all and the result was a complete absence of rowdiness. In the afternoon the crowds roamed indiscriminately, particularly in the High Street. In the evening the scenes were enlivened. For the first time in years the clocks on the Wallace Tower and the Steeple were working. The withdrawal of this particular restriction seemed likely to cause sore necks as the populace gazed aloft with a sense of novelty. Tramcars were now running in all the glory of their pre-war lights. Then something happened to disturb the idyll. This was the night when all the lighting restrictions were removed yet a temporary failure of the electric light in certain areas plunged a lot of people into darkness.

The removal of wartime restrictions was not yet total. Ayr United's next match was at Kilmarnock and, whereas the rail service was still intact, a restriction still persisted as to how many passengers could be carried. Demand heavily exceeded supply and the limited number of tickets got snapped up quickly. On the day of the match the Ayr support at Kilmarnock was considered to be as good as it would have been without the travelling restrictions. So how, apart from the comparative and lucky few, did they all get there? Many of them cycled. And the non-cyclists? This is what they did. They got a tram to the terminus at Prestwick Cross. Then they alighted and walked to Riccarton on the outskirts of Kilmarnock. From Riccarton they either continued walking to Rugby Park or completed the short final leg by tram. After watching Ayr United win 3-2 the whole process was reversed. Prestwick to Riccarton was a shorter distance in 1918 than it is now. It was more 'as the crow flies'. But the unalterable fact is that those hardy supporters had to put in an awful lot of footslogging. In return for a win at Kilmarnock the discomfort was worth it.

The quote you are about to read is beautifully written and it appeared in the *Ayrshire Post* in reference to the difficulties the supporters faced in getting to Kilmarnock. Your writer toyed with the idea of omitting it, lest there be accusations of repetition. I have previously reproduced this in the *Official History of Ayr United Football Club Volume One* (1990) and *Walking Down the Somerset Road* (2006). In truth it cannot be omitted from a book entitled *Ayr United At War*. Besides, how could anyone possibly tire of this truly wonderful piece of social commentary?

"The Kaiser has always been famous for the quality of the language he uses when in his high falutin moods, but the flow of flowery composition which was heard in the vicinity of Tam's Brig on Saturday about one o'clock surpasses anything the deposed Hun head was ever father of. The cause of the fiery outburst was the non-materialisation of a certain means of transport to Kilmarnock which had been promised to a coterie of rabid football enthusiasts."

With the Armistice signed, peace reigned over the land. Of course 'peace' in this context means the absence of fighting. The episode just described is illustrative of Ayr United supporters struggling to find an inner peace. This struggle stood to be passed on for posterity.

3

Some Characters of the Great War

The internment of John Cameron

Escape To Victory was an enjoyable yet ostensibly preposterous tale of famous footballers in captivity in wartime Germany. Where was the harm? Fiction is a frequent visitor to the world of wonderment. Yes, it was a world of wonderment. How else might one describe a story in which Bobby Moore, Pele and Ossie Ardiles were fellow captors who sought to counteract boredom by playing football in an encirclement of barbed wire and machine gun turrets? Had the film been ensconced in reality, inspiration might have been drawn from a barely documented true tale relating to the Great War.

When the Great War broke out there were British citizens who had the misfortune to find themselves trapped within German borders. Ruhleben, the site of a Berlin racecourse, became a prison camp for such citizens. Steve Bloomer of Derby County and England fame was one of them. Being England's most prolific goalscorer of his day, his fame ascended to legendary status. A fellow prisoner was John Cameron.

Cameron was an Ayr native whose father Kenneth was a grocer in Church Street. Initially he played juvenile football for Elmbank. He stepped up to play for Parkhouse. His final season there was 1894/95 by which time he was playing in the same forward line as Andy Aitken. In the 1895 close season Aitken was transferred to Newcastle United and in time he attained the captaincy of that club as well as Scotland. Cameron's transfer in the same close season took him, almost inevitably, to Queen's Park. His old and new clubs shared a mutual loathing of professionalism. On 28th March, 1896, he was one of four Queen's Park players in the Scotland team that drew 3-3 with Ireland in Belfast. That he moved to Everton was attributable to his job with Cunard and he accepted a professional contract solely due to a miscalculated business venture. He transferred to Tottenham Hotspur in the autumn of 1898 and was their top scorer in that first season. In 1899 he took on the role of secretary-manager whilst continuing as a player. His first success was in guiding Spurs to the Southern League championship in 1899/00. While still having non-league status he then steered and played for the club when they won the F.A. Cup in 1901. David Copeland, also a native of Ayr and a former Parkhouse player, played in that winning team. The complement of Ayrshire players was raised to four with the inclusion of Glenbuck natives Sandy Tait and Sandy Brown. In 1908 Spurs gained acceptance to the Second Division but John Cameron returned home to Ayr's Church Street in the same year. By then he had the accolade of being the first ever secretary of the Players' Union.

So how did it come about that he had a coaching assignment with Dresden FC which caused him to be ensnared in an enemy nation on the declaration of war? Speculatively it could be relevant that he would have had international connections through his career in shipping. Whatever the background to it he was rounded up with a vast number of British citizens and held in captivity at Ruhleben Racecourse on the outskirts of Berlin. What were known as barracks were, in truth, crudely improvised stables.

Cameron helped to organise football leagues within the camp and in 1915 he was the co-author of a 36-page camp football handbook. It listed 453 footballers of both amateur and professional status. His fellow author was Fred Pentland, formerly of Middlesbrough and England. Also influential in the creation of those leagues was the aforementioned Steve Bloomer who was caught up as a coach in Berlin. He was the most prolific goalscorer in England before Dixie Dean. There were two leagues comprising fourteen and thirteen teams. The 'barrack' team containing Bloomer was understandably dominant.

The act of interning in excess of 5,000 men in that location was an act of reprisal for Britain having already made captives of German citizens. Valiant attempts were made at easing their plight by organising sporting and educational pursuits. This was made possible by exploiting the pool of skills within the camp. As indicated in a letter sent by John Cameron in June 1916 there was still much to endure.

"Glad to say I'm keeping very well. The weather, until the last few days, has been simply vile – rain, rain, with a cold wind. This is the worst place for wind I ever struck. It beats the east coast hollow. Yesterday it came in thundering hot. Today it is about ninety in the shade, so you can imagine what life is like in a loft. Our constant cry is 'How long?' and we get utterly sick of each other at times. Must we be here for another football season? Surely not."

His concern about rain is emphasised by his repetition of the word. Yet his greatest concern was the future length of his captivity. Pertinently he was measuring time in football seasons.

In January 1918 it was learned that his name was listed in the latest batch of British civilians being repatriated. That month he was safely back in his home town and there was an understandable eagerness from people to find out a first-hand account of life in Germany. Having been held captive behind barbed wire, his knowledge of the privations of the German citizens was limited but he was in accord with so many others of those repatriated who testified that there was an extreme food shortage in the country. John Cameron was of the opinion that food conditions there might possibly cause a German surrender. His survival, and that of others, was a feat in itself.

"We should never have lived through it but for the parcels from home. While the esprit de corps was high, the strain on those who remain is severe, especially those of pedentary habit who have not been able to keep themselves fit by sports. I acted as secretary of the (camp) Football Association, and sometimes we had as many as eight league matches a day. Ragtime football, a loose kind of game for the elderly prisoners, kept many a man fit in spite of insufficient food."

In April 1918 Lawrence Gemson, motivated by ill-health caused by work pressure, retired as secretary-manager of Ayr United. This was convenient to the repatriation of John Cameron who took over the post after responding to this advertisement.

Ayr United Football and Athletic Club Limited

Wanted, secretary-manager – Applications, stating salary, and whether whole or part time can be given, to be lodged with Mr William Ferguson, 46 John Street, Ayr, on or before April 17th.

After one season he resigned, still not having recovered from the effects of being a prisoner. He moved to Leith to resume his career in shipping and died at his Easter Road home in April 1935.

His legacy was guiding Spurs from the Southern League to the Football League and being the architect of their first F.A. Cup win. He was the first occupant of the manager's office at White Hart Lane and could also claim to be in charge when the club first played in white shirts and navy shorts. To this it can be proudly added 'Born in Ayr'.

Alex Bennett – The mystery man

The pettiness of the Old Firm divide is risible to those of us with no inclination whatsoever towards either side. Bigotry, sectarianism and sheer blind hatred all comprise powerful reasons for steering clear and avowing loyalty to a provincial club. Admittedly an Ayr United versus Kilmarnock match is highly likely to offend those with delicate sensibilities. The difference is that we are now talking about local rivalry and the ill feeling is not entrenched in dubious conflicts dating back over the course of several centuries. It is difficult to inject sanity to a Rangers-Celtic debate. Attempts to do so are likely to be met with an order to 'go forth' (it is necessary to phrase this euphemistically).

Comparatively few players have been at both clubs, notwithstanding high profile examples such as Maurice Johnston and Kenny Miller. In the early part of the twentieth century Alex Bennett crossed the divide and it was just as contentious then as now. The distinguishing factor in Bennett's case was that he went on to play for Ayr United in odd circumstances.

At the age of twenty-one he moved from Rutherglen Glencairn to Celtic in 1903. He played for Celtic under the captaincy of Jimmy Hay, formerly of Ayr FC. Time would see him reunited under Hay's captaincy at Ayr United. From 1904/05 until 1909/10 inclusive, Celtic won six consecutive league titles. Playing as a forward Bennett was part of the first four of those successes. Further glory was bestowed upon him when he played in Celtic's Scottish Cup winning teams of 1907 and 1908.

During the 1908 close season he made the most unlikely move when signing for Rangers. Having scored twice against St. Mirren in the Scottish Cup final of 1908 he scored for Rangers against Celtic in the 1909 final. It was of no avail. The replay was level at the end and the crowd rioted on realising that no extra time would be played. In consequence the cup was withheld. With Rangers he won championship medals in 1910/11, 1911/12 and 1912/13. Seven championships divided between Celtic and Rangers! It was an exceptional career made even better by his eleven Scotland appearances. By the time of the Great War his stature in the Scottish game was huge.

For reasons of national security it was commonplace for players to appear under concealed names during the war. The scenario would occur when a player was guesting for a club in the area in which he was stationed. The practice was not universal. If there was deemed to be no threat to national security a player would simply guest under their actual name.

The Ayr United team versus Hibs at Somerset Park on 27th October, 1917, was: Lock, Bell, Brock, Hay, Somerville, McLaughlan, Middleton, Crosbie, "Thomson", Shankly and McNaughton. In a 2-2 draw the Ayr scorers were the Glenbuck men Johnny Crosbie and Alex Shankly (the eldest Shankly brother). Yet the focus of attention was on "Thomson", the centre-forward. The punctuation surrounding the name exposed the fact that it was an adopted name. In a report of this match he was discreetly referred to as "a once famous Glasgow centre-forward of international renown." That description would have provoked a puzzle in the mind of the reader. In the mind of anyone who attended the match there was nothing to solve. People instantly recognised Alex Bennett. The wider world may have remained unaware but it was always going to be a futile exercise to keep his identity a secret to those who were eye-witnesses. He was far too well known for that.

Bennett went on to complete nine league appearances for the club. His goals total amounted to nil but please consider this quote in the context of his debut: "He gave the men an object lesson in subjugating self for the good of his side when he let the ball go to Crosbie to score."

So how is it known that this player actually was Bennett? In January 1918 he was called up by the Rifle Brigade and there was a newspaper reference to A. Bennett being unable to play against his old club (Rangers) in the next match. The reference was fleeting and isolated yet without it this story could not have been told now.

A player of considerable stature donned the black and white hoops but even if you were to comb records with forensic scrutiny his name will not be found in any Ayr United line-up. The guise of "Thomson" persisted throughout all nine games.

His death on 11th January, 1940, was reported in the *Ayr Advertiser* by which time it was considered safe to use his real name!

Lawrence Gemson – The Heedie

Lawrence Gemson managed Ayr United in what remains the club's most successful league season ever. It happened at a time when he was combining football duties with his day job as a headmaster. He combined so much more and gradually succumbed to the effects of too much work. It would not be overly speculative to suggest that there really were not enough hours in the day for this man.

Life began for him in Preston in 1873. In 1881 his father George took over the family pub, The Rose, Shamrock and Thistle in the town's Bridge Street but by 1891 the Gemsons had moved to Glasgow. At the age of twenty-one Mr Gemson moved from Glasgow to St.Mary's College in Hammersmith where he underwent teacher training. On his return to Glasgow he began to teach at St.Mary's Catholic School and that was where he made the acquaintance of Tom Maley who had played in Celtic's first ever team along with his brother Willie. The relationship he fostered with the Maleys was to prove most advantageous to the future Ayr United.

On 9th October, 1899, Lawrence Gemson moved to Ayr in order to take over the role of headmaster of St.Margaret's. The role remained unrelinquished until his retirement in 1933. The longevity theme can be maintained to tell you that his good friend Willie Maley managed Celtic from 1897 until early in 1940.

The Ayr Schools Football Association was founded in 1908 and Mr Gemson was chairman from 1910 until 1914. As an eminent figure in the Roman Catholic Church he became president of the Catholic Young Men's Society of Scotland. An equal eminence in education allowed him to become a Fellow of the Educational Institute of Scotland and president of the West of Scotland Catholic Teachers' Association. A further attainment was a directorship of Ayr County Hospital.

On the evening of 14th March, 1910, Tom Maley delivered a lecture in Ayr's Carrick Street Hall. Alluding to the gathering momentum of amalgamation talks between Ayr FC and Parkhouse he said: "It has always seemed strange to me why Ayr does not have a First League club. I think it strange that that there is not one really good club – a club that could make a strong claim for admission to the First League. When I heard that amalgamation was proposed I rejoiced and said that it was indeed a wise, proper and prudent step. If all the considerations are carefully weighed up I am sure that the matter of amalgamation will not be long delayed."

His last point was prophetic. The amalgamation to form Ayr United was concluded on 9th May, 1910. Lawrence Gemson became a director in 1911 and greatly assisted the club by utilising his connections with the Maleys. Borrowing players from Celtic was an exercise undertaken almost at will. The best was Willie McStay who, as an eighteen-year-old left-back, came to Ayr on loan in November 1912 and remained until the 1916 close season. His great nephew Jock McStay was to become an Ayr United player in 1996. Another outstanding loanee was Joe Cassidy. In periods ranging from one game to several years they came. It is a fact that goalkeeper John Thomson, before his ascent to legendary status, even played two matches for Ayr United reserves in December 1926.

There was a hint of betrayal when Ayr United played a league fixture at Clydebank on 29th September, 1917. McInally, Hyslop and Brodie were all on loan from Celtic in that match despite Willie Maley's brother Alec being the manager of Clydebank at the time.

The mention of Willie, Tom and Alec Maley now prompts mention of the fourth Maley brother, the only one not actively employed in football. Charles, the eldest of the brothers, was the priest at St.Margaret's in Ayr. He was a regular occupant of the directors' box at Somerset Park and his death in November 1917 saw the Ayr United club flag flown at half-mast for a match against Dumbarton. Another prominent Roman Catholic who enthusiastically supported the club was Canon Collins. When he passed away in April 1915 the club flag had also flown at half-mast, the occasion being a match against Dundee.

The credentials of Lawrence Gemson were clear. He was clever, committed and well connected but with no discernible record in professional football it might be wondered how he became manager of Ayr United. His earliest passion for the game is easy to trace. It was fostered in Preston in the 1880s. In 1889 Preston North End was the first club to win the league championship and F.A. Cup double.

In the closing weeks of season 1914/15 Herbert Dainty's role as player-manager became the subject of some enforced revision. As a centre-half he was still acquitting himself well at the age of thirty-six, although opposing fans and players were apt to experience distaste at his liking for hard-tackling. On the managerial side he could also reflect satisfactorily with the club on course for a fifth-place finish, beaten for fourth place only by Morton having a superior goal average. Celtic and Rangers were beaten at Ayr on consecutive Saturdays and, by virtue of beating them at Ibrox Park, full league points were extracted from Rangers. So why, in late March 1915, was there speculation about him transferring to Raith Rovers? Quite simply it was because he had a business in Dundee. The *Ayr Advertiser* proffered the view that: "There is no probability of him going to his old club due to a vendetta with the Dens Park crowd. Dainty will never again don a dark blue shirt. Dundee Hibs would gladly sign him but he wants first class football." He would have donned a dark blue shirt had he moved to Raith Rovers but the assertion that he would never again wear the dark blue shirt of Dundee was correct. This was despite him playing in their Scottish Cup winning team of 1910. The misgiving about first class football was proven wayward when, in April 1915, he went to Dundee Hibs, also as player-manager.

In time for season 1915/16 Lawrence Gemson's role as a director doubled up with that of secretary-manager. Despite his eminence in religious and academic fields his credentials for a job in football management were severely lacking. In daytime hours he still had a school to run quite apart from the considerable matter of the committees he served on. Headmasters were colloquially known as 'The Heedie'. How could a Heedie cope in football management? The school was a short walk away in Whitletts Road, notwithstanding a time when it was relocated after being requisitioned by the army. Compounding the convenience was Mr Gemson's house being in Somerset Road, right next to the ground. What of team selection? At the time it was the domain of the entire board. Yes, the board! That was the selection process regardless of the experience or inexperience of the incumbent. Tactics were the preserve of the experienced players in the team. In 1915/16 Ayr United fielded a total of seven players who were past or future Scotland internationalists. They were Willie McStay, Jimmy Hay, Neil McBain, Willie Cringan, Johnny Crosbie, Jimmy Richardson and Joe Cassidy. (Richardson's appearances were in unofficial Victory internationals). It was a deep pool of tactical awareness. Had it not been for the difficulties visited upon the club by the war, Mr Gemson would not have been subject to the remotest of consideration for management. He was a man of virtue thrust into a results-driven environment, albeit that adverse results were liable to incur public wrath directed at the board rather than the manager. Adverse results were a rarity in 1915/16. By finishing fourth in the league a club record was created which remains unbeaten. Dolefully it could be pondered whether it will ever be beaten. The next two seasons were rendered miserable by the constraints of war. Fifteenth place out of twenty was the club's lot in 1916/17 and in 1917/18 it was the wooden spoon. When the 1917/18 season was drawing to its lamentable close Mr Gemson announced that he was retiring from his job as secretary-manager. The reason cited could almost have been guessed. It was ill-health caused by work pressure. His resignation extended to his directorship but he was reinstated to the board in 1922 and became chairman in 1923.

At the time of his Golden Wedding in January 1947 a special blessing was received from Rome and on 30th January, 1950, he died at the age of seventy-six in his Somerset Road home. How apt that he passed away in immediate proximity to the club he had served so well by utilising his connections, serving on the board and taking on the management during the Great War.

He was survived by his wife Ann, who died on 23rd August, 1952, at the age of seventy-six. He also left two daughters and a son. His daughters, Anne and Alice, were still regular attenders at Somerset Park in the 1970s at which time they still stayed in the Somerset Road home. Anne passed away at the age of seventy-five on 19th August, 1975, and Alice died at the age of seventy-one on 10th February, 1978. When they were engaged in conversation on a match day they were proud to tell you: "Our Dad used to be the manager here."

Sam Aitken – Blinded in battle

War memorials are a justifiable tribute to those men who have fallen in war. It is only right that their names should be recorded for posterity and that we should remember them each year on armistice day. Yet when we are remembering the fallen it would be remiss to omit tribute to those who were so badly injured in battle as to have a major impact on what remained of their lives. Lives? Perhaps it would be more fitting to use the word existence.

Sam Aitken played in the first ever Scottish League match at Somerset Park. The date was 4th September, 1897. Ayr FC lost that 2nd Division match 4-1 to the Govan-based

Linthouse but the occasion was historic. The old ground has hosted league football ever since with the exception of the years between 1940 and 1945. At the end of that 1897/98 season he was the club's top scorer with fourteen goals in the seventeen league games played out of a possible eighteen. His conversion from inside-forward to centre-half had the effect of stunting his opportunities for scoring in future seasons but he did excel in that position and in May 1903 he was transferred to Middlesbrough.

In August 1912 he was back at Somerset Park after being transferred from Raith Rovers to the two-year-old Ayr United club. In an outstanding season for player and club the 2nd Division championship was retained. Sam Aitken was willing to apply himself. This we know from a report of a league match played at Johnstone on 15th March, 1913. The field was described as "worse than any pitch we have ever seen." Inappropriately the ground name was Newfield! In the *Ayrshire Post* it was written that: "In the last minutes Sam Aitken did not have a white spot on his face."

After enlisting for the Great War, he found quagmires many times worse than the one at Johnstone and he was now living under the fear of death. He did survive the war but he was left virtually blind.

His plight came to the attention of R. S. McColl, the former Queen's Park and Scotland centre-forward (and founder of the confectionery chain bearing his name). McColl assembled an X1 to play an Ayr Select at Beresford Park on 24th May,1924. It was a benefit match for Sam Aitken.

R. S. McColl XI - R. S. McColl (Queen's Park), Henry (Manchester City), Garden (Queen's Park), Bowie (Rangers), Campbell (Rangers), Roberts (Queen's Park), Jarvis (Stoke City), John McMenemy (Celtic), Raitt (Third Lanark), J. McMenemy (Celtic) and T. N. McColl (Queen's Park).

Ayr Select: Massey (Ayr United), Miller (Parkhouse), A. Aitken (Ayr FC), White (Ayr FC), Gillespie (Ayr United), McLaughlan (Ayr United), Hamilton (Ayr FC), Massie (Ayr

FC), Phillips (Parkhouse), Cameron (Parkhouse) and Lindsay (Ayr FC).

Most of the players on the field had long since retired from playing. Just look at those mentions of Ayr FC and Parkhouse and bear in mind that this was 1924. R. S. McColl was aged forty-eight and playing as a goalkeeper. His actual position had been centre-forward. The exertions were too much for Charlie Phillips who walked off early in the game to be replaced by Galbraith (Parkhouse).

The visitors won 3-1 before a crowd of around 2,000. It hardly mattered. It was all in a good cause. Although it did matter to the old Ayr FC player Gladstone Hamilton who accidentally kicked the ground and got taken to hospital with a broken leg.

On Friday, 7th March, 1930, Sam Aitken passed away. Only in death was he able to cast off his legacy of the war. That legacy was almost total blindness. On the next day the flag flew at half-mast at Somerset Park. As a further mark of respect the Ayr United team wore black mourning armlets while inflicting a 3-1 defeat on Airdrie.

Samuel Mitchell Aitken died at his home address of 43 Oswald Road, Ayr. On 24th April, 1991, I visited that house to speak to Archie Buchanan, then aged ninety-one. Mr Buchanan had managed Ayr United from January 1926 until September 1931, and he remains the club's youngest ever manager. He told me that he had stayed there since June 1930 thereby succeeding Sam Aitken as the occupant. Mr Buchanan was lucky to miss service in the Great War. At the age of eighteen he was called up by the Highland Light Infantry but the armistice came in time to prevent service in France.

4

The Second World War

The future is definitely not ours to see. This adage was ringingly endorsed after Ayr United got relegated from the Premier Division in 1978 and I predicted a return by 1979. In truth it was more than a prediction. It was an assumption. There was not the slightest glimmer of doubt. Not only did this supposed cast iron certainty not materialise then, neither did the return materialise as the years rolled into a new century and beyond. History now testifies that it was a bad forecast. Now have a look at this excerpt from the *Ayrshire Post* dated 16th September, 1938.

"The Nazis have made the Germans a strong and subtle people, bound by the strongest racial ties. That could never have been achieved without Adolf Hitler. What a man! Giving his all to Germany and getting nothing but a job as Chancellor. He left his native Austria and gave up everything to save Germany from her enemies. Then he came home and saved Austria from her enemies. Such a man has a great future. Rudolf Hess stands right behind Hitler. Heinrich Himmler controls the Gestapo. They are all fine boys, inspired by lofty ideals and wouldn't fight. They are the world's greatest peace lovers, and it is shameful how other peoples on the earth provoke them. Their patience is an outstanding virtue, and the kindness of their hearts finds expression in a hundred and one little acts of toleration and consideration towards those who do not agree with them."

The same edition of that newspaper carried the story of an Ayr youth, just back from Germany. Lured by the glowing accounts in guide books, he had gone to the Rhineland for a hiking holiday. One day he wandered into an area where military manoeuvres were taking place. He saw trucks laden with troops, soldiers manning machine gun posts and guns camouflaged by the branches of trees. With complete naivety he chatted away to some of the soldiers while the crackle of machine gun fire resonated in the background. He got arrested but was released after cross-examination but this episode did not sit comfortably with the opinion about "the world's greatest peace lovers."

Approaching the end of September 1938, war with Germany had become more than a possibility. After the Great War, some national borders were redrawn, thus causing a lot of Germans to be effectively displaced in that part of Czechoslovakia known as the Sudetenland. Hitler wished to annexe the Sudetenland. The threat that such aggression could escalate into war was taken so seriously that advertisements were placed for people to work in a quickly-formed Air Raid Precautions Service in Ayr.

On 27th September there was an ominous tone at a meeting of Ayr County Council. They discussed such chilling topics as first-aid posts, gas masks and the supply of food. The convenor of the A.R.P. committee even ventured to say: "It is conceivable that war may break out before any further meeting of the County Council can be held."

The local papers in Ayr gave extensive information on how to build your own air raid shelter. There were also tips on how to look after your gas mask and advice was given not to hoard food. The hopes of averting conflict lay with Prime Minister Neville Chamberlain who had agreed to a meeting with Hitler, Mussolini and Daladier. The world paused in anticipation of knowing whether peace would be brokered at Munich on 29th September.

The international situation was woven into a report of a match ending Ayr United 3 Hearts 1 on 24th September.

"The international situation almost took a back seat on Saturday night. War clouds were temporarily forgotten, the tension and anxiety of the crisis relegated to the background. Ayr people wore a grin that even an air raid could not wipe off. Who cared for rumours of hostilities? Why worry if peace trembled on the brink? Away with dull care! Let it rain, snow or hail! – or even Heil! For Ayr United had beaten Hearts. The victory was a topic of conversation on Saturday night. The name on everyone's lips was not Hitler. It was Marshall!"

The crux of this was easy to grasp. Britain seemed to be teetering on the brink of war but the world was a beautiful place anyway because Ayr United had won. This was that wonderful world of perspective.

Your writer is in possession of a letter hand-written by Jimmy Marshall. It is dated 24th November, 1987, and was posted to Somerset Park. He specifically mentioned this match against Hearts, modestly omitting mention of his goal. He gave the team as: Hall, Dyer, Strain, Taylor, Currie, Mayes, Craig, Dimmer, Yardley, Gemmell and Marshall. Ross, rather than Taylor, played at right-half but you will agree that ten out of eleven was an outstanding recollection forty-nine years after the match.

On 30th September Neville Chamberlain returned from Munich. After stepping down from the plane he made his famous "peace in our time" speech. The supposed peace agreement had averted war. Germany annexing part of Czechoslovakia was not something Britain considered worthy of fighting over. It transpired that the Munich peace agreement was worthless. Hitler had lied about not making further territorial demands. Within several weeks he began to plan a full scale invasion of the whole of Czechoslovakia and in March 1939 the plan was executed. It was correctly anticipated that Poland would be a future victim of similar German aggression. Britain made a bold stance to the effect that war would be waged were that to happen.

At the Ayr United annual general meeting in 1939 Andrew Wright was appointed chairman and David Govan became vice-chairman. On 7th June, Tom Steen, the former Ayr United director and outstanding administrator, died at Dumfries, his last years being blighted by bankruptcy. As treasurer of the S.F.A. during the Great War, he had made an outstanding contribution in steering the Scottish game through that conflict. In the near certainty of another war happening, any future reshaping of our game would also have an Ayr United director as an influential participant. That man was Douglas Bowie, the S.F.A. president from 1937 until 1945.

The clichéd comment relating to the summer of 1939 was that the war clouds were gathering. In concise terms this was true. On 15th July a batch of 150 "embryo militiamen" reported to Ayr Barracks. It was considered that these men were making history because "they were the first to enter the barracks of an army raised in peace time for the maintenance of peace."

On the evening of 25th July, all twenty-two Ayr United players reported to Somerset Park to resume pre-season training. Between then and the season's opening league fixture Terry McGibbons returned to the fold. Between seasons 1933/34 and 1937/38 he had scored 118 league goals for the club in 173 appearances. He was transferred to Preston North End in the 1938 close season and was now returning to his native Irvine to resume his Ayr United career. His return was fated to terminate after five matches, all of which were later declared void. Jacky Cox, a native of Darvel, also quit Preston North End to join Ayr United prior to the start of season 1939/40. He was a hard-tackling half-back whose senior debut for Hamilton Accies had been at Ayr in the opening fixture of season 1931/32. Cox would ultimately become club manager in 1956.

For acquiring players of such calibre, the Ayr United board got commended for their bold policy. After the opening league match, a 5-0 defeat away to Albion Rovers, it was condemnation rather than commendation.

The signs were ominous. During the last week in August, painters were busy in Ayr. Their task was to paint corners and crossings to guide drivers in the event of a blackout

Terry McGibbons - The outbreak of the Second World War brought a premature end to his senior career.

being imposed in response to fears of air raids. Then came an announcement that all schools in Ayrshire would be closed for at least a week. This was to facilitate the evacuation process whereby approximately 44,000 children were being sent to the county from the areas of Scotland perceived to be at greater risk from air raids.

With Germany preparing to invade Poland it was a time of suspense in the knowledge that this eventuality would precipitate Britain towards a state of war. On 1st September, 1939, a Friday, the invasion did take place. The chances of maintaining peace were too small to contemplate.

There is a true adage that people can remember where they were when they heard that John F. Kennedy had been assassinated. The author can give personal testimony to this. In a similar fashion, younger generations can instantly recall the time when the Twin Towers went down. By the same principle, Ayr United supporters were easily able to recall the match played on the eve of the Second World War being declared.

That match was a First Division fixture at home to Hamilton Accies. Ayr's 6-1 win also helped in preserving the memory. The *Sunday Mail* carrying the now famous date of 3rd September, 1939, was heavy in war connotations in relation to this match. The twin headline was: SHOCK AIR RAIDS ON ACCIES: CLARK GETS IN THREE DIRECT HITS. Jacky Clark, nicknamed 'Elkie', had signed his Ayr United contract on 4th May, 1939, and it was valid until 30th April, 1940. His terms of £4 per week during the playing season seemed well worth the money for a player who could score a hat-trick at this level after stepping up from Rutherglen Glencairn. Yet his contract and those of his colleagues were soon to be void.

On the morning of 3rd September, the British Ambassador in Berlin handed an ultimatum to the German Government clarifying that unless they stated an intention to withdraw their troops from Poland, a state of war would exist between the two countries. The deadline for acceptance was 11 a.m.

This was the background to Neville Chamberlain's radio announcement from 10 Downing Street at 11.15 a.m. The crux of the message was: "I have to tell you that no such undertaking has been received and that consequently this country is at war with Germany."

The future of Scottish football was dealt with summarily as evidenced by this terse statement.

"The Scottish Football Association informed enquiring clubs on Monday that in view of the Government Order closing all places of entertainment and outdoor sport, football players' contracts are automatically cancelled. The Scottish League is of the opinion that contracts are merely suspended but the question chiefly concerns the S.F.A."

Being a full-time club, the players were due to show up at Somerset Park on the Tuesday as usual, Monday being the normal day off. Many of them had already been in contact before then in order to ascertain the position. They were all out of work and there was no scope for negotiation. On Friday, 8th September, the Home Secretary issued an order that clubs in neutral districts would be allowed to play friendly matches. In the perceived areas of risk, football was to be banned. In Scotland the banned areas comprised Glasgow, Edinburgh, Dundee, Dunfermline and Clydebank. Mr J.C. Lyon, the chairman of Hamilton Accies, concocted an idea in which clubs in Lanarkshire, Renfrewshire and Ayrshire would adopt a club from a risk area for the duration of the war and share the ground on alternate weeks. He found insufficient support.

The weeks passed by with no resumption of football. On 18th September, the plan to resume the Scottish League programme was suspended during a conference between the S.F.A. and League officials. After the meeting it was tersely stated: "A deputation has been appointed to interview the Secretary of State for Scotland with a view to the removal of all restrictions on football." The Government remained fearful of the vulnerability of large crowds in the face of air raids. They stated that crowds at competitive matches should not exceed 50% of seating capacity. On that basis Somerset Park would have been restricted to just under 700.

Douglas Bowie headed the joint Scottish Football Association and Scottish Football League deputation to London. As a major S.F.A. office bearer and Ayr United director, his mission mirrored that of Tom Steen back in 1914. This time the deputation had an hour-long meeting with John Colville, the Secretary of State for Scotland. The other delegates were James Bowie, president of the Scottish League, J.S. Murray, president of the Scottish Junior F.A., William McAndrew, secretary of the Scottish League and George Graham, secretary of the S.F.A. The situation was fully discussed but the real purpose of requesting the meeting was to plead for a lifting of some of the restrictions to a greater or lesser extent. Note the conciliatory tone. This implies that the removal of all restrictions had since been deemed too much to ask for. In 1914 there had been conflicting interpretations on the outcome of the talks. There was no scope for the same eventuality in 1939 because the meeting was concluded with no indication given as to what would or would not happen.

When political approval was forthcoming it was deemed appropriate to recommence football on a regional basis. Subject to the approval of the member clubs, it was expected that competitive football would start again by the end of October. The proposal was to divide the country into two sections.

Southern and Western: Albion Rovers, Ayr United, Celtic, Clyde, Hamilton Accies, Kilmarnock, Motherwell, Partick Thistle, Queen of the South, Rangers, St. Mirren, Third Lanark, Airdrie, Dumbarton, Morton and Queen's Park.

Northern and Eastern: Aberdeen, Alloa Athletic, Arbroath, Cowdenbeath, Falkirk, Hearts, Hibs, St.Johnstone, Dundee, Dundee United, Dunfermline Athletic, East Fife, King's Park, Leith Athletic or St.Bernard's, Raith Rovers and Stenhousemuir.

Left out: Brechin City, East Stirling, Edinburgh City, Forfar Athletic, Montrose and either Leith Athletic or St.Bernard's.

There were seven votes against the proposal. With an apology for stating the obvious, the dissenters were the five excluded clubs and the two involved in the 'either or' situation. It was proposed that a levy would be placed on the participating clubs in order to help meet the rents and rates of those excluded. This did nothing to soothe the ire of those frozen out. An assurance that they would retain the rights of membership did not placate these clubs either. It left the Forfarshire Association apoplectic at the prospect of losing three of its six member clubs. Local opinion in that area was consensual that it would be disastrous. It was reasonably argued that no other county was being asked to make a similar sacrifice. The Forfarshire Association put forward a plan for three sectional leagues – West, East and Midlands. It was given no consideration at all. What of the Edinburgh clubs Leith Athletic and St.Bernard's? Which one was it to be? A request for them to amalgamate was refused and St. Bernard's got included.

An early war casualty was James Croall who had once played for Parkhouse. His career, initially as a full-back and later as an inside-forward, further included Rangers, Alloa Athletic, Falkirk and Chelsea. He played in Falkirk's Scottish Cup winning team of 1913 and made three Scotland appearances. When his days playing for Chelsea were over he became a teacher in London. In 1939 he was a master at Holland Street School in the Lambeth District. For obvious reasons the evacuation of children from that area was a priority. James Croall accompanied a party of evacuees from London to the eminently safer environs of South Petherton in Somerset. One day he went missing. A week later (on 18th September) it was discovered that he had drowned in the River Parrett. There is a sombre irony that he died at the age of fifty-four after a move that was made for reasons of safety. Yet it is appropriate to mention that Lambeth was bombed heavily.

Ayr United's first match since the outbreak was the replayed final of the Ayrshire Cup, held over from the season before. The Somerset Park crowd was about 4,000 or nearer 5,000 depending on which newspaper you cared to believe. For a Saturday afternoon, either figure was an endorsement that the demands of the forces and war work had already conspired to stunt the turnout. Curtailed public transport was another debilitating factor. With a 3-1 result Ayr United retained the trophy. There was a rebuke for the supporters of both sides.

"Despite the repeated requests over radio and the national press for the general public to carry their gas masks, especially to places of entertainment including sports meetings, those who carried out the request were in the minority at Somerset Park. Time is not far distant when it will be made compulsory for everyone to carry respirators on all occasions. Though danger of gas attack in Ayrshire is highly improbable it is nevertheless not impossible."

The Ayrshire Yeomanry practising cavalry charges on the beaches of Ayr comprised another symbol of these extraordinary times. Five years later they were to do it in gory reality when storming the beaches of Normandy as the 151st Field Regiment, Royal Artillery. Students of military history may be interested to know that they converted to artillery in 1940.

At a special meeting of the Scottish League clubs it was decided that the new set-up would begin on 21st October. Players were not permitted to get paid more than £2 per week and no bonuses were to be allowed. There was also a stipulation that home clubs had to meet a £50 guarantee for visiting clubs. Since most of the Ayr United players were now working during the day, the club set the training schedule for Tuesday and Thursday nights. Those who did not live in the town were permitted to train at other grounds.

The terms of a recently issued Government announcement compelled the military registration of players aged between twenty and twenty-two. It meant that this applied to literally half of Ayr United's squad of twenty-two registered players. They were Craik, McConnell, Newall, Smith, Whiteford, Clark, Kirkland, Alex Stewart, Albert Stewart, Craig and Marshall. Given the high potential for the unavailability of players, the staging of the Scottish 2nd XI Cup may have seemed inadvisable. With the first round scheduled for the Saturday before the commencement of the Regional League, it was an immediate priority. The potential problem was tempered by allowing first teams to compete.

So far only Peter Smith had departed on military service. Whereas Smith would return, Terry McGibbons was fated never to play for the club again. Then aged twenty-seven, he became occupied in the more pressing matter of shipyard work and had ceased playing on the abandonment of the First Division programme. He remains Ayr United's all-time second highest scorer of league goals but this legend of a player was reduced to playing for the Ayrshire Dockyard team through the intervention of war. This was a man who, in 1938, had played for Preston North End against Arsenal in a Charity Shield match at Highbury.

MORTON DEFIED THE AYR RAIDS. Thus a clichéd headline conspired with a war connotation to describe the opening Regional League match, the occasion of a 1-0 defeat at home to Morton.

The scarcities of the last conflict were expected but better administration of the rationing system promised to cut down queues. That was the plan but then we all know what Rabbie Burns said about the "best laid plans." By October the shops in Ayr were struggling to supply adequate quantities of butter. That was the bad news. The good news was that the Patna Flyer was back. Tommy Robertson was a winger with lightning pace. If proof is required then you may be told that he was a Powderhall sprinter. He played for Ayr United between 1929 and 1934 then he was transferred to Dundee. In 1936 he was transferred to Clyde and he played in their Scottish Cup winning team of 1939. On 3rd November, 1939, he signed for Ayr United again and was in the team against Rangers in the Regional League the next day. One week later Fally Rodger was back playing for Ayr United too. He played at outside-left, the opposite wing from Robertson. Rodger had made his Ayr United debut in 1931 and was sold to Manchester City in 1935. In 1938 he moved to Northampton Town. Upon his release in the summer of 1939 he returned to his native Ayr. He trained at Somerset Park and offered his services as a player but he was quick to stress that he only wished to play in the event of a player shortage, unselfishly preferring not to displace any regular member of the team. Well, the time had now come. Fally's reintroduction to the team coincided with the Ayr United debut of George Hamilton, an inside-forward of sublime skill. He was a native of Irvine who started out with Irvine Meadow, subsequent moves taking him to Queen of the South and Aberdeen. Because he was now back working in Irvine, Ayr United managed to obtain his services on loan.

Traditionally Ayr United have monopolised local sporting interest but there was intense competition in 1939. The Ayr Raiders ice hockey team played at the ice rink in Beresford Terrace and their league showed none of the restraints of regionalisation that were imposed on football. The other teams in their league were Fife Flyers, Perth Panthers, Dundee Tigers, Dunfermline Vikings and Falkirk Lions. Although not playing especially well at the time, a crowd estimated at 4,000 appeared for their home match with Falkirk on the night of 10th November, when they won 7-4; on the following Friday about 1,000 people were turned away. Thankfully their matches were all scheduled for Friday nights.

During the Great War the problem of getting a team on the field was addressed by a relaxation of the rules to the extent that clubs could field whosoever they chose. This flexibility enabled the acquisition of players of other clubs who happened to be billeted or working in proximity to the local area. Here in 1939 the League Management Committee

Frank Thompson - The Ayr United manager when the club ceased for the duration of World War Two.

did adopt special rules to deal with the emergency situation but the flexibility was less than total. It was permitted to use Anglo players though they still had to be registered. In November, Ayr United and the Stirling-based King's Park were fined for playing unregistered players.

Bitter experience obliterated any "all over by Christmas" predictions although in December Sir Thomas Moore, the local Member of Parliament, made so bold as to suggest that it would end in 1940. Whereas he supported his argument by sound reasoning it can be said that he was erring heavily on the side of optimism. In retrospect this phase of the hostilities was referred to as "the phoney war". Hostilities? Nothing threatening seemed to be happening. The anticipated attacks from the air had not taken place. The R.A.F. had undergone missions to Germany but they had simply dropped propaganda leaflets. It was merely the lull before the storm.

On the morning of a match at Dumbarton, Jimmy Craik, Hugh McConnell, Jock Newall and George Hamilton all had to register for military service. Albeit that the people did not feel imperilled, there was still a depression in the air. The mood was succinctly captured in the *Ayrshire Post*.

"Since the eventful days of the last great war that brought untold suffering to the world, no Christmas has been celebrated under such gloomy conditions as the one just past."

For Ayr United supporters serving with the British Expeditionary Force in France, there was a nice Christmas gift. They had written to the club asking for a ball. Manager Frank Thompson happily obliged. On the Home Front depression, rather than fear, reigned. The blackout did a great deal to intensify the winter gloom. Locally and nationally it was causing a high number of road accidents. Blacked-out windows on the Ayr buses left people clueless as to whether or not they had reached their stop. Counting the stops or relying on guesswork were the wholly unsatisfactory solutions.

James 'Henry' Hall - Custodian of the Ayr United goal at the outbreak of World War Two.

Jacky Clark hit a goalscoring consistency. He struck a hat-trick in a 3-3 draw at Motherwell on 6th January, 1940. Including the voided match on the eve of war, it was his fourth hat-trick of the season. His regular job at this time was as a bricklayer. Occupations of other Ayr United players then were: Jimmy Hall – engineer; Jimmy Dyer – coal salesman: Jimmy Craik – agricultural blacksmith; Davy Currie – postman; Jacky Cox – shipyard worker; George Hamilton – shipyard worker; Jock Whiteford – coalminer; Tommy Robertson – engaged in work of national importance; Fally Rodger – joiner; Lewis Thow – in the glass trade. It was apparent that some were in reserved occupations and, in the meantime at least, would be immune from the call-up.

Club trainer Eddie Summers was now in the Army as was Jock Newall who had been called up by the Royal Engineers. Hugh McConnell was now in the R.A.F. William Sneddon, formerly of Rutherglen Glencairn, Falkirk, Brentford and Swansea Town, was a half-back signed to replace Newall. In the immediate term he would play one game which preceded a run of postponements then his enlistment in the R.A.F. His career with the club only extended to two more games while on leave in March.

Sneddon signed on a Friday night and made his debut at Celtic Park the next day. To put it mildly, team selection was rendered problematical when Hall and Whiteford called off with flu. Currie was therefore switched from left-back to centre-half which happened to be his natural position anyway. Dyer made the switch from right-back to left-back and Craik occupied the right-back position. The issue of replacing goalkeeper Hall was supposedly resolved by Frank Thompson in a phone call to Donald Turner, his counterpart at Partick Thistle, on the Friday night. On the Saturday Ayr United arrived at Glasgow by train. True to his word Donald Turner was at the station along with Johnstone, the Partick Thistle goalkeeper. An ominous confab then took place prior to a hitch emerging. The outcome was the party heading for

Celtic Park without a goalkeeper. On arrival there was no sign of Jacky Clark. Then he arrived, having finished his work at 1p.m. Ex-Ayr United goalkeeper Bob Smith, then of Dundee United, looked into the Ayr dressing room. Ideal! Well, it would have been ideal had it not been too late to get clearance for him to play. The goalkeeping options were narrowed down to Fally Rodger, Davy Currie and Jimmy Dyer. Fally Rodger was then chosen. William Sneddon scored from a free-kick in the opening minutes. Jacky Clark scored twice to take it to 3-0 and when Celtic got a goal with fifteen minutes remaining, the visibility was so bad that Gould "seemed to be" their marksmen but there was a distinct lack of certainty. In a 3-1 win Jacky Clark had scored twice after completing his shift as a bricky then making a frantic dash to the ground. Yet he was eclipsed for publicity by Fally Rodger. With the score at 1-0 he saved a penalty from Willie Lyon and was generally outstanding. Fally remains one of three Ayr United outfield players to save a penalty when pressed into goalkeeping action in an emergency. The others were Jimmy McLeod at Alloa on 9th February 1926 and John Robertson at Dundee on 18th April, 1998.

"Supporters of Ayr United who intend travelling to Greenock on Saturday are advised to take their gas masks with them. They will not be admitted if they do not. Be warned and take your respirator."

That particular warning left no room for doubt. The Morton match was postponed anyway yet that did not diminish the relevance of the message that was increasingly being put out. It was the first of three consecutive Saturdays on which postponements were made. Blackouts were instrumental in tempering the public mood and now there was a whiteout. The picture in Ayr reflected that throughout Scotland. It was estimated that 35,000 to 40,000 tons of snow fell on Ayr in January 1940. The volume was considerable in view of the fact that the first snowfall did not land until the 18th. With a heavy frost as an additional ingredient, football did not stand a chance of taking place. Communications in the district were practically at a standstill. A notice outside the Western S.M.T. bus station in Ayr stated: All Roads Are Closed. Local buses still ran but there was not even a road link to Glasgow. Maybole and the surrounding villages existed in a state of isolation and it was the same further south in communities such as Barr, Barrhill and Colmonell. In Ayr there was an apathetic mood about the absence of football. During pre-war times, postponements caused great discussion but the question had now to be asked as to whether football had lost its appeal. What would happen now? The fixture backlog could only be made up by scheduling matches for midweek or extending the season. Midweek games were disliked by the Government, although ultimately they did happen in 1939/40. The fear of midweek football was linked to the danger of air raids. Of course this could have implied that the Luftwaffe operated strictly on a Monday to Friday basis!

Some clubs were now beginning to discuss whether they could afford to carry on. In more minor grades a lot had already taken the decision to cease for the duration. With dubious timing a plan emerged for the setting up of a national cup competition. It was the subject of disagreement. The S.F.A. wanted to include the clubs frozen out of the regional set-up whilst the Scottish League wished only to include the clubs who were in that set-up.

On the morning of a match against Clyde at Shawfield, Jock Whiteford and Jacky Clark registered for the forces, thus rendering them in a state of suspense pending the arrival of the brown envelope that would signify the call-up.

On the last Saturday in February the national cup competition began. With total certainty you can be told that it was not slickly named. It was called the Scottish Cup Emergency Competition. However the first round draw did succeed in addressing the question of local apathy with football. It was to be Kilmarnock versus Ayr United with the double appeal of a two-legged format. In the first leg Tommy

Robertson had to retire from the field with a knee injury. This was the Patna Flyer's last appearance in an Ayr United shirt. Losing 1-0 at Rugby Park was creditable with ten men for eighty-three minutes. On the next Saturday 9,941 plus season ticket holders congregated inside Somerset Park for the second leg. Tommy Robertson's replacement was Tony Carroll, once of Clyde and more recently with Luton Town. Carroll was now in business in Glasgow. He may have replaced Robertson as a winger but he would never match him as a sprinter. After a 2-2 draw culminated in an aggregate defeat, the *Ayrshire Post* and the *Ayr Advertiser* (it must have been a freelance report) had this to say: "When Carroll, Ayr's new outside-right from Luton Town wears off some of his superfluous fat, he will be an attraction at Somerset Park." This was actually written in a serious context. In war time the game was always apt to throw up examples of eccentricity and this was one of them. Compounding that eccentricity was the fact that supporters of this time call him 'Beer Barrel Carroll' and the name was passed on for posterity.

Jimmy Marshall was the next to enlist and the season was going completely awry according to this summary of a 2-0 loss away to St. Mirren.

"The big disappointment was centre-forward Clark. He has lost his capacity for scoring goals. He is now engaged in nightshift work involving a long shift on the Friday night which ends at six o'clock on Saturday morning. In war days football clubs have just to accept such situations. Gates are down, big staffs cannot be carried and jaded players cannot be given a rest."

On the morning of a match at Dumfries, Hyam Dimmer registered for military service. An injury to Jimmy Hall (known as Henry Hall after the band leader) led to Tom Brown playing in goal against Queen of the South on that day. Brown was registered with Ipswich Town at this time and he travelled to the game from a training base "somewhere in Scotland." The secrecy of his location had to be described in the language of censorship. In time the story emerged that he was in the Commandos. The war was to see him parachuted into China to help the guerrillas who were fighting the Japanese. It was a one-off appearance in April 1940 but he rejoined the club in December 1945. We can rest assured that his potentially lethal adventures would have left him with no nerves about guarding the Ayr United goal in that post war phase.

April 1940 brought worrying developments. The Germans invaded Norway and Denmark. Ostensibly this was done to afford protection to these countries. The people of Britain were not so gullible as to believe this. Where would their all-conquering armies be directed next?

Closer to home there was a very large symbol of the war. The Admiralty put a minefield in the Firth of Clyde. It stretched all the way from the Kintyre Peninsula in Argyllshire to the Ayrshire coast. At its northern limit it extended to twenty-three miles. At the southern end it stretched to twenty-five miles. It completely blocked the entrance to the Firth. Vessels entering or leaving the Firth had to obtain instructions for safe passage from either the British naval or Consular authorities.

With the Regional League winding towards an inglorious close, Ayr United remained second bottom, a position that would remain intact. Rangers and Queen of the South vied for the title. You need hardly be a student of Scottish football to correctly surmise that Rangers were on course to win it. Celtic struggled heavily yet even in war time our game was cloaked with the inevitability that one or other of the Old Firm would take the lion's share of the honours. Rangers went on to win the title in all six of the Southern and Western Regional League campaigns. During the Great War Celtic won every First Division title with the exception of the last one which they lost narrowly to Rangers. Such is the tedious nature of our game.

Jacky Clark's scoring record was inconsistent with the team's overall status as strugglers. He was on course to score twenty-six goals in the twenty nine out of thirty Regional League games in which he played. It was remarkable when balanced against his work schedule and the toiling nature of the team's progress.

Andy McCall returned to the club somewhat late in the day. He was a stylish wing-half who departed in 1935 and had played for St.Johnstone and Huddersfield Town. On the evening of 30th April, 1940, he agreed to help out his old club. He was registered with Nottingham Forest at this time. It was a brief reunion covering the second last of the two remaining Regional League games as well as the semi-final and final of the Scottish 2nd XI Cup. Please recall that this cup competition involved first teams in this makeshift season. Queen of the South, Kilmarnock and Celtic were beaten to reach the final. Aberdeen matched that success in the Northern and Eastern area to become the other finalist.

To say that the course of the war was becoming critical does not fully convey the extent of the danger. Holland, Belgium and Luxembourg quickly fell to the German invaders. Where next? France of course. Neville Chamberlain relinquished his position as Prime Minister. In metaphorical terms it could have been said that Winston Churchill, the new incumbent, had to hit the ground running (albeit that this is a modern buzz phrase). How soon, in actual terms, would it be before German paratroopers would be hitting British ground running?

In the face of it all there were still people willing to discuss the shape of Scottish football for 1940/41. With new age groups being called up, player availability would continue to be a concern. Or would it? That premise was based on there still being a war to fight. The Germans were now over the French border. It was considered that the Maginot Line would have halted any such advance. This was a massive fortification built by the French along the length of their border with Germany. Well, almost along the length of the border. In the north it was thought that the Ardennes area

Andy McCall - He returned to Ayr United briefly in 1940.

was so impenetrable as to act as a natural barrier to an invading German army. The Germans proved it not to be impenetrable and they simply went round the Maginot Line. Their advance was rapid when it swung westward towards the channel ports. These were nervous times as evidenced by the following appeal by the chief warden of the Ayr A.R.P.

"We are at the present moment engaged in a life and death struggle. The war in Holland and Belgium may at any moment be brought to our very doors. Henceforth we cannot for an instant ignore the fact that every life in our native land is in jeopardy and that the chief bulwark of safety lies in a common performance of duty. Everyone who fails in that endangers not only himself but his fellow citizens. There are 480 trained wardens in Ayr, all of whom are voluntary workers. I now want another hundred men to take up their duties along with these wardens. It is necessary that the warden should live near his warden's post so volunteers will only be asked to serve in their own districts. I make this appeal with confidence for it is unthinkable that, when all is at stake, it should not be answered."

Neither was the paranoia about Fifth Columnists conducive to a mood of calm.

The concept of opportunistically burying bad news is a modern one. In the thick of all this a massive financial loss was reported at the Ayr United annual general meeting but we should not establish any correlation. The timing was coincidental. For the financial year ending 31st March, 1940, the loss was £2,674 : 11s : 3d. The source of this devastating deficit was easy to trace. The gate receipts for that period totalled £6,052 : 19s : 8d. That was less than half of the amount for the corresponding period the year before.

On 24th May the enemy took Boulogne. On 27th May they took Calais. On the Saturday between those dates (25th) Ayr United played at Aberdeen in the first leg of the Scottish 2nd XI Cup final. With the country in a genuine state of emergency it was little wonder that the journey was fraught with delays.

The train broke down near Forfar and it took an hour to get it moving again. It was necessary for the players to get changed on the train. Even at that and with the aid of taxis at Aberdeen, the team got to Pittodrie ten minutes after the advertised kick-off time. Jimmy Dykes, Hearts' international half-back, made his third Ayr United appearance in this tie, having been acquired on loan earlier in the month. In normal times it would have been difficult to acquire a player of such calibre. The same applied to George Hamilton who was back on familiar soil at Aberdeen. Thomson of Hamilton Accies played at left-half and the only other game he played for Ayr was in the second leg of this tie. Lewis Thow gave the team the lead in a 1-1 draw but his place in the second leg was doubtful because, on the Wednesday between, he underwent a medical examination for the forces. Ultimately he did play.

BRITAIN NEVER IN GREATER PERIL – This headline was contained within the edition of the *Ayr Advertiser* that reported the match at Aberdeen. It was not written in the hysterical manner of today's tabloid excess. In excess of 330,000 British and French troops were trapped on the beaches in and near to Dunkirk. The British Expeditionary Force was threatened with annihilation. One of them was Ayr United's Jock Newall who had last played for the club on 6th January, just prior to his call-up to the Royal Engineers. With the aid of a veritable armada of small boats, a huge-scale catastrophe was averted. After the war Newall was not fit enough to resume his football career and he allowed eighteen months to pass before putting his boots on again. By 1952 he was a footballing legend – in New Zealand! In that year a newspaper in that country described him as "one of New Zealand's greatest soccer forwards." As a teenager he had originally signed for Ayr United from Burnfoothill Primrose in the summer of 1936, his father Tom having played for Ayr in the Second Division championship season of 1912/13. Jock Newall scored twenty-eight goals in seventeen games for New Zealand during tours of the Pacific in 1951 and 1952. He survived Dunkirk by a considerable distance, dying in his native Scotland at the age of eighty-six in 2004.

With the Dunkirk evacuation in progress at the time, Ayr United and Aberdeen took to the field on 1st June, 1940, to battle for custody of the Scottish 2nd XI Cup. With the aggregate score level and first teams competing the crowd would have been considerable in different circumstances. That the attendance did not top 3,000 was attributed to it being a time of stress and anxiety. Jock Pattillo (25) scored for Aberdeen. Seemingly unhandicapped by his immense bulk, Tony Carroll levelled it a few minutes before half-time. Fally Rodger (84) made it 2-1 on the day and it was a 3-2 aggregate win.

The cup would normally have been presented by Alex Jackson, the president of the 2nd XI Association. Since he was an Ayr United director the duty was delegated to the treasurer, John Kelly of Celtic. The presentation took place inside but chairman Andrew Wright had the presence of mind to come out and exhibit the trophy to the waiting crowd. It evoked memories of the trophy being won by Ayr Strollers back in 1888.

Andrew Wright commented: "Football for next year is in the lap of the Gods." By the time this comment was reported there was another statement. "Ayr United is closed down until further notice."

The decision to close down coincided with director David Murray being named as an honorary secretary. His grandson, of the same name, made a high profile bid to wrest control of the club in 1988 before turning his attention on Rangers.

Several times down through the years I have spoken to supporters who were around in 1940. Did the club make the right decision to close down for the duration? There appeared to be consensus that it was definitely a wrong decision. David Govan quit the board in protest. Andrew Wright also opposed the closure. On a point of principle he resigned the chairmanship but stayed on the board.

When the town clocks chimed the start of 1945 the crowds were, in relative terms, muted. The celebrations, if they could even have been called that, were easily the quietest of any New Year since the war began. There was an entire absence of drunkenness although this was largely down to the scarcity of whisky rather than any pretence at restraint. The picture in Ayr was mirrored across the southern part of the county.

Since 1940 weeds had been growing on the terracing at Somerset Park despite the place being in continued use. Two of the local junior clubs, Newton Rovers and S.S. and E. Athletic (Scottish Stamping and Engineering), used the ground on alternate Saturdays for their home fixtures in the Western League. Whitletts Victoria, founded in 1944, had their own ground at Voluntary Park and were to gain admission to the Western League in 1945/46. The occasional schools match was played on the war time Somerset Park as were some high profile representative matches. These were R.A.F. versus The Army (1941) and Scottish Command versus Western Command in 1944, 1945 and even in 1946. All of these games were staged on New Year's Day. The 1945 match was attended by about 8,000, there being the considerable lure of seeing the aspiring Billy Wright and the already accomplished Tommy Lawton. Hyam Dimmer, formerly a flamboyantly brilliant Ayr United inside-forward, was a spectator at this game. Officials of Newton Rovers opportunistically had talks with him while the action was in progress and he agreed to sign. What a scoop! He was a long way from the end of his career. In the post war years he played for Fulham, Aldershot and Bristol City. In March 1945 the eccentricities of war time were illustrated by a Newton Rovers versus Ayrshire Dockyard match in which Hyam Dimmer opposed Terry McGibbons, another Ayr United legend. The word legend has not been applied lightly.

By February people had justification for entertaining the notion that the hostilities were coming to an end. The Red Army pressed towards Berlin from the east while the British and Americans pressed from the west. Of course the war had also to be won on another front. An artillery regiment recruited from Ayr, Kilmarnock, Irvine and Dumfries was fighting with the 36th Division in Central Burma.

On 14th February, Liverpool released half-back Matt Busby. On the same date a report emerged that he had been fixed up as manager of Ayr United. The club officially denied the report. Manchester United historians are in accord that Busby declined the Ayr job. It can be concluded that either the Ayr board pursued an interest at a later date or these historians have based their information on a wrongly reported piece of information. In October 1945 he began to rebuild Manchester United. The Busby Babes are now written large in history.

At least the story hinted that the club would be revived. There were still players on the retained list who could be recalled but the conclusive proof that Ayr United would soon be back came in March when Annbank United goalkeeper Alex Corbett was signed on a provisional form. Volunteers from the Ninth Holding Battalion, based at Ayr Racecourse, moved in to tackle the weeds on the terracing and a move was made to derequisition Somerset Park from the A.R.P. who had been using the showers and sprays for cleansing purposes.

By April, winning the war in Europe was so certain that Ayr Town Council discussed the victory celebrations. Or rather they didn't! In retrospect it may seem inconceivable that the council members were opposed to the prospect of any great displays of celebration. When the *Ayrshire Post* reported this stance the heading to the story was AYR TOWN COUNCIL NOT TO ENCOURAGE JOLLIFICATION. The townsfolk were traditionally adept at staging a peace celebration as had been shown in 1902 and 1918. Why were they being asked to exercise restraint in 1945? Bailie Lanham most eloquently summed up why in the following terms.

"After all is said and done, the cessation of hostilities in Europe will not mean the end of the war; we have still a serious part of the war to tackle in the Far East. I feel that there are many citizens who have every reason to deprecate any celebrations on the occasion of the end in the West while we still have the Far East job on our hands. Many have friends, husbands, sons and relatives fighting out there and they would not entirely welcome any widespread celebration on such an occasion."

Fair point! The hub of this was not meanness of spirit. It was out of respect for our lads still fighting the Japanese in Burma. By way of compromise it was decided that, when the time inevitably came, flags would be put out and the council members would attend a thanksgiving service in the Auld Kirk.

Liberated prisoners were arriving home whilst VE Day edged nearer. On 2nd May the Germans surrendered in Italy. When Berlin finally fell under the weight of the Red Army it was all over.

The unconditional surrender of the German land, sea and air forces in Europe was announced by Winston Churchill in a broadcast on the Tuesday afternoon of 8th May. So did the people of Ayr comply with the 'no jollification' advice? They did to a certain degree. Confusion about the timing of the official announcement and no relaxation in the dim-out restrictions managed to take the edge off the euphoria. The flags were out, the bells were rung and dancing was staged on the Low Green but the celebrations were localised rather than happening at one particular focal point. The town bell rung and naval ratings paraded in the High Street. In the evening the Salvation Army band marched down the High Street before assembling at the Fish Cross to continue playing. The considerable matter of the conflict in the Far East no doubt preyed on the mind.

Season 1945/46 was designed on the basis of an A Division of sixteen clubs and a B Division of fourteen clubs. The generation of fans annoyed at the closure in 1940, suffered equal annoyance at the set-up instigated here in 1945. To call it a fix would be an understatement. In placing Ayr United in B Division, the seven men responsible took no cognisance of the final league positions in the last peacetime season. James Bowie presided over the carve-up. He should not be confused with Ayr United director Douglas Bowie who, in the previous month, had not sought re-election after eight years as president of the Scottish Football Association. The other men complicit in this treachery comprised three delegates from the disbanding Northern and Eastern League and three from the disbanding Southern and Western League. This was Scottish football in 1945 – the world of the phantom promotion and the world of relegation with no grounds other than self interest.

On 20th June it was announced that Bob Ferrier, the former Motherwell winger, would be the new manager on a full-time basis. First of all he had to disentangle himself from his employment in Dumbarton and his part time position as manager of Airdrie.

At the club's annual general meeting a debit balance of £5,567 was reported. A post war attendance boom lay ahead, without which this could have been critical.

The Town Council had been using the club's dressing rooms for A.R.P. cleansing purposes. With the premises now derequisitioned, the club was asked to submit any claim they had for damage caused. With a hint of opportunism the club replied that they had no claim provided that they were allowed to keep the showers and sprays that had been installed for the A.R.P. This was agreed.

Strenuous efforts were made to restore Somerset Park to its pre-war glory. Oversized weeds were removed from the terracing, fresh coats of paint were applied and the general tidy-up continued until the place looked spruce. But the country still remained at war with Japan.

On 6th August an atomic bomb was dropped on the Japanese city of Hiroshima. On 9th August the same fate befell the Japanese city of Nagasaki. It seems gloriously out of context to relate that the week concluded with Ayr United losing 3-0 at home to Airdrie in the inaugural B Division fixture on Saturday, 11th August. A crowd in the region of 6,500 saw the first Ayr United game in more than five years. The team was: Alex Corbett, Jimmy Dyer, David Henderson, S.W.Smith, Jock Whiteford, Peter Smith, Jimmy Melvin, Albert Stewart, John Malcolm, Jimmy Leitch and Bert Harper. By the time of the next match the war was over in its entirety.

VJ Day was Wednesday, 15th August. Prime Minister Clement Attlee made a broadcast at midnight and in categorical terms the people were told of Japan's unconditional surrender. The VJ Day announcement was not marked by the hesitation and uncertainty prevalent on VE Day. The war was over beyond all shadow of a doubt. The public had been given just ten minutes notice that Mr Attlee was going to make an announcement. Those who had not retired for the night quickly took to the streets to waken their neighbours. This time the 'no jollification' recommendation did not apply. Neither was there a dim-out. Ayr's streets were fully illuminated. The ships in the harbour sounded their sirens and this was the cue for cars and buses to make what noise they could. Some people unashamedly took to the streets in their night attire. It was a warm night anyway. Bonfires were lit in South Harbour Street, King Street and Waggon Road. There was no particular focal point. Throughout the town groups of people linked arms and celebrated with unrestrained joy. The seafront attracted many. Verey lights were fired to spectacularly light up the water. The pipe band of the 9th Holding Battalion emerged from their billet at the racecourse. This was one occasion when a pipe band parading the streets in the early hours of the morning would not be complained about.

"Never could the streets have been the scene of such joy unconfined as was witnessed from shortly after midnight until between five and six o'clock in the morning as civilians of all ages and service men and women rejoiced that World War 2 had become history and was no longer a present menace."

This was the testimony of someone who witnessed it.

Peace prevailed and Ayr United were back.

Norrie McNeil became a rock at the heart of the Ayr United defence when the club started to rebuild after the Second World War. At representative level in the Army he played with and against legends of the British game.

5

Afghanistan

Researching the minutiae of life in a combat situation can only go so far in helping to articulate what it was really like for our service people. First-hand accounts tend to conform to a pattern reliable enough to give us an idea but we can barely begin to imagine the innermost thoughts and concerns of those faced with life and death situations. My father saw active service in France, Belgium, Holland and Germany yet the only stories he passed on for posterity were humorous interludes. This illustrates the default setting of the combat soldier. It may be out of respect for fallen comrades but the anecdotes of war often err towards the lighter aspects of life. This tale of Andy Connell falls gloriously into that category.

An inhospitable terrain and a fanatical enemy in the Taliban; suffice to say that Afghanistan is not the type of place you would want to be without a good reason. Well there was a good reason for being there. Our service personnel were sent to do their bit to help rid the world of terrorism. But can you honestly think of a worse place to be? On the next page is a visual aid to help you ponder that question.

This is Andy in Kandahar in 2007. He was serving as an R.A.F. medic at the time. In no particular order he has a clear allegiance to Ayr United and his country. Just as clear is his non-allegiance to the town of Ayr United's enemy. Totally endorsing the point he made this quote: "Afghanistan may be a total hellhole but it still beats Killie."

The Boer War, the Great War, the Second World War and Afghanistan all carry stories which prove that thoughts

Andy Connell

have drifted to Somerset Park from the most horrendous of places. But Andy's stunt left one unanswered question. Was he kidding?

Another tale of Afghanistan in relation to Ayr United would have no credibility were it not for the photographic evidence. Tabloid newspapers have a love affair with lists. In clichéd style we can expect to be regaled with *20 Things You Didn't Know About . . .* (insert celebrity name of choice). The fact that all but three of the things are already in the public domain and the rest are inconsequential seems not to matter. So, entering into the spirit, here are a couple of things you probably did not know about David Beckham.

1. In May 2010 he visited Camp Bastion.
2. Whilst there he showed his true football allegiance!

There is no mistaking the guy on the left. For Ayr United supporters there is no mistaking the guy on the right either.

He is Michael Green. As a Warrant Officer Class 1 he was given the job of looking after the illustrious visitor. Refreshingly Michael had this to say of the great footballing icon: "He had absolutely no airs and graces."

At the start of this book football's capability of transcending major conflict was alluded to. The pages you have since read will have borne a heavy endorsement. If there is any lingering doubt just think about Michael Green packing his Ayr United scarf before heading out to fight Taliban insurgency.

David Beckham and Michael Green

Fixtures

Ayr FC's record during the Boer War.
1899/00

Date	Match	Competition	Venue
19/08/1899	Ayr FC 1	Port Glasgow Athl. 3	2nd Division	Somerset Park.
26/08/1899	Airdrie 5	Ayr FC 2	2nd Division	Broomfield Park.
02/09/1999	Ayr FC 1	Linthouse 5	2nd Division	Somerset Park.
09/09/1899	Ayr FC 1	Beith 2	Scottish Qualifying Cup 1st round	Somerset Park
16/09/1899	Morton 7	Ayr FC 1	2nd Division	Cappielow Park.
23/09/1899	Partick Thistle 4	Ayr FC 1	2nd Division	Meadowside.
30/09/1899	Ayr FC 1	Annbank 3	Ayrshire Cup 1st round, 1st leg	Somerset Park.
07/10/1899	Ayr FC 2	Hamilton Accies 1	2nd Division	Somerset Park.
14/10/1899	Ayr FC 0	Leith Athletic 1	2nd Division	Somerset Park.
21/10/1899	Ayr FC 2	Partick Thistle 1	2nd Division	Somerset Park.
28/10/1899	Ayr FC 1	Annbank 2	Ayrshire Cup 1st round, 2nd leg	Pebble Park.
04/11/1899	Ayr FC 2	Motherwell 4	2nd Division	Fir Park.
11/11/1899	Ayr FC 2	Linthouse 2	2nd Division	Govandale Park.
18/11/1899	Airdrie 1	Ayr FC 2	2nd Division	Somerset Park.

Abandoned after 65 minutes due to bad light.

| 25/11/1899 | Abercorn 3 | Ayr FC 3 | 2nd Division | Ralston Park. |
| 02/12/1899 | Leith Athletic 3 | Ayr FC 1 | 2nd Division | Hawkhill. |

09/12/1899	Ayr FC 1	Abercorn 2	2nd Division	Somerset Park.
16/12/1899	Hamilton Accies 0	Ayr FC 4	2nd Division	Douglas Park.
23/12/1899	Ayr FC 1	Morton 4	2nd Division	Somerset Park.
30/12/1899	Ayr FC 5	Airdrie 0	2nd Division	Somerset Park.
02/01/1900	Ayr FC 3	East Stirling 1	Scottish County League	Clune Park.
06/01/1900	Port Glasgow Ath. 2	Ayr FC 8	2nd Division	Somerset Park.
27/01/1900	Ayr FC 4	St. Mirren 3	Friendly	Merchiston Park.
03/02/1900	East Stirling 2	Ayr FC 0	Scottish County League	Somerset Park.
17/02/1900	Ayr FC 2	Motherwell 1	2nd Division	Stark's Park.
03/03/1900	Raith Rovers 2	Ayr FC 2	Scottish County League	Somerset Park.
31/03/1900	Ayr FC 2	Maybole 3	Friendly	Somerset Park.
07/04/1900	Ayr FC 6	Hamilton Accies 4	Scottish County League	Somerset Park.
14/04/1900	Ayr FC 3	Raith Rovers 1	Scottish County League	Douglas Park.
21/04/1900	Hamilton Accies 2	Ayr FC 2	Scottish County League	Fir Park.
28/04/1900	Motherwell 3	Ayr FC 2	Scottish County League	Somerset Park.
05/05/1900	Ayr FC 1	Abercorn 2	Scottish County League	Ralston Park.
12/05/1900	Abercorn 0	Ayr FC 3	Scottish County League	

Scottish League Second Division

Played	Won	Drawn	Lost	For	Against	Points
18	6	2	10	39	48	14

Position eighth.

1900/01

16/08/1900	Ayr FC 1	Galston 3	Friendly		Somerset Park.
18/08/1900	Ayr FC 2	Annbank 1	Friendly		Somerset Park.
25/08/1900	Ayr FC 4	Hamilton Accies 2	2nd Division		Somerset Park.
01/09/1900	East Stirling 2	Ayr FC 1	2nd Division		Merchiston Park.
08/09/1900	Ayr FC 6	Hurlford 1	Scottish Qual. Cup 1st round		Somerset Park.
15/09/1900	Ayr FC 1	Abercorn 0	2nd Division		Somerset Park.
22/09/1900	Annbank 0	Ayr FC 2	Scottish Qual. Cup 2nd round		Pebble Park.
29/09/1900	Ayr FC 3	Kilmarnock 3	Ayrshire Cup 1st round, 1st leg		Somerset Park.
06/10/1900	Galston 2	Ayr FC 4	Scottish Qual. Cup 3rd round		Riverside Park.
13/10/1900	Ayr FC 1	Port Glasgow Athl. 0	2nd Division		Somerset Park.
20/10/1900	Ayr FC 1	Kilwinning Eglinton 0	Scottish Qual. Cup 4th round		Somerset Park.
27/10/1900	Kilmarnock 1	Ayr FC 3	Ayrshire Cup 1st round, 2nd leg		Rugby Park.
03/11/1900	Ayr FC 5	Douglas Wanderers 1	Scottish Qual. Cup qu-final		Somerset Park.
10/11/1900	Ayr FC 5	Airdrie 1	2nd Division		Somerset Park.
17/11/1900	Ayr FC 1	St.Bernard's 0	2nd Division		Somerset Park.
24/11/1900	Ayr FC 1	Stenhousemuir 2	Scottish Qual. Cup semi-final		Somerset Park.
01/12/1900	Ayr FC 8	Hurlford 0	Ayrshire Cup 2nd round, 1st leg		Somerset Park.
	It was later agreed to scrap the second leg.				
08/12/1900	Ayr FC 3	Motherwell 1	2nd Division		Somerset Park.
				/Scottish County League	
15/12/1900	Airdrie 5	Ayr FC 4	2nd Division		Broomfield Park.
29/12/1900	Port Glasgow Athl. 5	Ayr FC 0	2nd Division		Clune Park.
01/01/1901	Ayr FC 3	Clyde 2	2nd Division		Somerset Park.
05/01/1901	Leith Athletic 4	Ayr FC 1	2nd Division		Hawkhill.
12/01/1901	Ayr FC 2	Orion 2	Scottish Cup 1st round		Somerset Park.

182

19/01/1901	Orion 1	Ayr FC 3	Scottish Cup 1st round replay	Cattofield.
26/01/1901	Ayr FC 1	St. Mirren 3	Scottish Cup 2nd round	Somerset Park.
09/02/1901	Kilwinning Eglinton 3	Ayr FC 1	Ayrshire Cup semi-final, 1st leg	Blacklands Park.
16/02/1901	Ayr FC 2	Kilwinning Eglinton 0	Ayrshire Cup semi-final, 2nd leg	Somerset Park.
23/02/1901	Ayr FC 1	Leith Athletic 0	2nd Division	Somerset Park.
02/03/1901	Ayr FC 1	Kilwinning Eglinton 0	Ayrshire Cup semi-final replay	Warner Park (Stevenston).
09/03/1901	Motherwell 2	Ayr FC 1	2nd Division	Fir Park.
16/03/1901	Abercorn 2	Ayr FC 1	2nd Division	Ralston Park.
23/03/1901	Ayr FC 1	Stevenston Thistle 1	Ayrshire Cup final	Rugby Park.
30/03/1901	Ayr FC 2	Stevenston Thistle 1	Ayrshire Cup final replay	Rugby Park.
06/04/1901	Ayr FC 3	East Stirling 2	2nd Division	Somerset Park.
13/04/1901	Clyde 2	Ayr FC 1	2nd Division	Shawfield.
27/04/1901	St.Bernard's 1	Ayr FC 0	2nd Division	Powderhall.
04/05/1901	Ayr FC 1	Annbank 1	Ayr Charity Cup semi-final *after extra time*	Somerset Park.
08/05/1901	Ayr FC 2	Annbank 2	Ayr Charity Cup semi-final replay	
11/05/1901	Hamilton Accies 3	Ayr FC 1	2nd Division	Beresford Park.
13/05/1901	Ayr FC 5	Annbank 1	Ayr Charity Cup semi final, 2nd replay	Douglas Park. Beresford Park.

Scottish League Second Division

Played	Won	Drawn	Lost	For	Against	Points
18	9	0	9	32	34	18
Position	sixth.					

1901/02

17/08/1901	Abercorn 5	Ayr FC 2	2nd Division	Ralston Park.
24/08/1901	Ayr FC 2	Hamilton Accies 0	2nd Division	Somerset Park.
31/08/1901	St.Bernard's 4	Ayr FC 1	2nd Division	The Gymnasium Ground.
07/09/1901	Ayr FC 8	Girvan 1	Scottish Qual. Cup 1st round	Somerset Park.
14/09/1901	Ayr FC 1	Arthurlie 0	2nd Division	Somerset Park.
19/09/1901	Ayr FC 1	Celtic 1	Friendly	Somerset Park.
21/09/1901	Ayr FC 5	Parkhouse 1	Scottish Qual. Cup 2nd round	Somerset Park.
28/09/1901	Kilwinning Eglinton 0	Ayr FC 1	Ayrshire Cup 1st round, 1st leg	Blacklands Park.
05/10/1901	Beith 0	Ayr FC 6	Scottish Qual. Cup 3rd round	Muirfield.
12/10/1901	Leith Athletic 1	Ayr FC 1	2nd Division	Hawkhill.
19/10/1901	Kilwinning Eglinton 3	Ayr FC 1	Scottish Qual. Cup 4th round	Blacklands Park.
26/10/1901	Ayr FC 5	Kilwinning Eglinton 1	Ayrshire Cup 1st round, 2nd leg	Somerset Park.
02/11/1901	Arthurlie 0	Ayr FC 1	2nd Division	Dunterlie Park.
09/11/1901	Ayr FC 2	Partick Thistle 2	2nd Division	Somerset Park.
16/11/1901	Ayr FC 1	Airdrie 1	2nd Division	Somerset Park.
23/11/1901	Ayr FC 2	Galston 1	Ayrshire Cup 1st round, 1st leg	Somerset Park.

The second leg was postponed twice then Ayr FC withdrew.

30/11/1901	Ayr FC 1	Clyde 0	2nd Division	Somerset Park.
07/12/1901	Hamilton Accies 4	Ayr FC 1	2nd Division	Douglas Park.
02/01/1902	Ayr FC 1	St.Bernard's 0	2nd Division	Somerset Park.
04/01/1902	Ayr FC 3	Leith Athletic 1	2nd Division	Somerset Park.

11/01/1902	Ayr FC 0 Dundee 0	Scottish Cup 1st round	Somerset Park.
18/01/1902	Dundee 2 Ayr FC 0	Scottish Cup 1st round replay	Dens Park.
25/01/1902	Clyde 1 Ayr FC 0	2nd Division	Shawfield.
01/02/1902	Port Glasgow Athl. 3 Ayr FC 0	2nd Division	Clune Park.
22/02/1902	Ayr FC 1 Port Glasgow Athl. 1	2nd Division	Somerset Park.
01/03/1902	Ayr FC 0 East Stirling 1	2nd Division	Somerset Park.
08/03/1902	Partick Thistle 2 Ayr FC 0	2nd Division	Meadowside.
15/03/1902	Ayr FC 3 Abercorn 0	2nd Division	Somerset Park.
22/03/1902	East Stirling 0 Ayr FC 1	2nd Division	Merchiston Park.
29/03/1902	Airdrie 3 Ayr FC 2	2nd Division	Broomfield Park.
05/04/1902	Ayr FC 2 Motherwell 2	2nd Division	Somerset Park.
12/04/1902	Ayr FC 2 Annbank 1	Friendly	Somerset Park.
19/04/1902	Motherwell 2 Ayr FC 1	2nd Division	Fir Park.
03/05/1902	Ayr FC 2 Kilwinning Eglinton 0	Ayr Charity Cup semi-final	Beresford Park.
10/05/1902	Ayr FC 2 Annbank 0	Ayr Charity Cup final	Somerset Park.
14/05/1902	Maybole 4 Ayr FC 4	Friendly	Ladywell Park.
17/05/1902	Ayr FC 1 Kilmarnock 1	Ibrox Disaster Fund	Somerset Park.

Scottish League Second Division

Played	Won	Drawn	Lost	For	Against	Points
22	8	5	9	27	33	21
Position	eighth.					

Ayr United 1914/15

15/08/1914	Ayr United 4	Partick Thistle 0	1st Division	Somerset Park.
19/08/1914	Kilmarnock 4	Ayr United 4	Andrew Cunningham's testimonial	Rugby Park.
22/08/1914	Hamilton Accies 2	Ayr United 1	1st Division	Douglas Park.
29/08/1914	Ayr United 0	Airdrie 0	1st Division	Somerset Park.
05/09/1914	Dumbarton 1	Ayr United 2	1st Division	Boghead Park.
12/09/1914	Ayr United 1	Aberdeen 0	1st Division	Somerset Park.
19/09/1914	Kilmarnock 1	Ayr United 2	1st Division	Rugby Park.
21/09/1914	Hearts 1	Ayr United 0	1st Division	Tynecastle Park.
26/09/1914	Ayr United 0	St. Mirren 2	1st Division	Somerset Park.
03/10/1914	Hibs 0	Ayr United 4	1st Division	Easter Road.
10/10/1914	Ayr United 1	Celtic 0	1st Division	Somerset Park.
17/10/1914	Ayr United 2	Rangers 0	1st Division	Somerset Park.
24/10/1914	Third Lanark 2	Ayr United 1	1st Division	Cathkin Park.
31/10/1914	Ayr United 0	Hearts 2	1st Division	Somerset Park.
07/11/1914	Falkirk 1	Ayr United 1	1st Division	Brockville Park.
14/11/1914	Ayr United 2	Morton 1	1st Division	Somerset Park.
21/11/1914	Celtic 4	Ayr United 0	1st Division	Celtic Park.
28/11/1914	Queen's Park 1	Ayr United 1	1st Division	Hampden Park.
05/12/1914	Ayr United 3	Raith Rovers 0	1st Division	Somerset Park.
12/12/1914	Dundee 2	Ayr United 3	1st Division	Dens Park.
19/12/1914	Ayr United 2	Dumbarton 1	1st Division	Somerset Park.
26/12/1914	Morton 3	Ayr United 0	1st Division	Cappielow Park.

02/01/1915	Ayr United 1	Third Lanark 0	1st Division	Somerset Park.
04/01/1915	Ayr United 2	Hibs 1	1st Division	Somerset Park.
09/01/1915	Aberdeen 1	Ayr United 1	1st Division	Pittodrie.
16/01/1915	Motherwell 1	Ayr United 1	1st Division	Fir Park.
30/01/1915	Partick Thistle 2	Ayr United 0	1st Division	Firhill Park.
06/02/1915	Ayr United 2	Queen's Park 1	1st Division	Somerset Park.
13/02/1915	Rangers 1	Ayr United 3	1st Division	Ibrox Park.
20/02/1915	Ayr United 2	Kilmarnock 0	1st Division	Somerset Park.
27/02/1915	St. Mirren 1	Ayr United 3	1st Division	St. Mirren Park.
06/03/1915	Ayr United 1	Falkirk 2	1st Division	Somerset Park.
13/03/1915	Ayr United 1	Motherwell 1	1st Division	Somerset Park.
20/03/1915	Clyde 3	Ayr United 1	1st Division	Firhill Park.
27/03/1915	Ayr United 2	Hamilton Accies 0	1st Division	Somerset Park.
03/04/1915	Raith Rovers 0	Ayr United 0	1st Division	Stark's Park.
10/04/1915	Ayr United 0	Dundee 0	1st Division	Somerset Park.
17/04/1915	Airdrie 1	Ayr United 2	1st Division	Broomfield Park.
24/04/1915	Ayr United 3	Clyde 1	1st Division	Somerset Park.
28/04/1915	Ayr United 4	Kilmarnock 2	Friendly	Beresford Park.
08/05/1915	Ayr United 5	Queen's Park 3	Ayr Charity Cup final	Somerset Park.

Scottish League First Division

Played	Won	Drawn	Lost	For	Against	Points
38	20	8	10	55	40	48

Position fifth.

1915/16

21/08/1915	Dundee 2	Ayr United 0	1st Division	Dens Park.
28/08/1915	Ayr United 2	Hibs 3	1st Division	Somerset Park.
04/09/1915	Dumbarton 0	Ayr United 3	1st Division	Boghead Park.
11/09/1915	Ayr United 1	Hamilton Accies 0	1st Division	Somerset Park.
15/09/1915	Ayr United 4	3rd Glasgow Highlanders 5 For Military Funds		Beresford Park.
18/09/1915	Rangers 5	Ayr United 2	1st Division	Ibrox Park.
25/09/1915	Aberdeen 1	Ayr United 1	1st Division	Pittodrie.
02/10/1915	Ayr United 1	Raith Rovers 1	1st Division	Somerset Park.
09/10/1915	Hearts 0	Ayr United 5	1st Division	Tynecastle Park.
16/10/1915	Ayr United 3	Motherwell 2	1st Division	Somerset Park.
23/10/1915	Kilmarnock 0	Ayr United 1	1st Division	Rugby Park.
30/10/1915	Third Lanark 1	Ayr United 1	1st Division	Cathkin Park.
06/11/1915	Ayr United 1	Morton 1	1st Division	Somerset Park.
13/11/1915	Airdrie 3	Ayr United 1	1st Division	Broomfield Park.
27/11/1915	Ayr United 0	Partick Thistle 0	1st Division	Somerset Park.
04/12/1915	Falkirk 1	Ayr United 0	1st Division	Brockville Park.
11/12/1915	Ayr United 0	Celtic 4	1st Division	Somerset Park.
18/12/1915	St. Mirren 1	Ayr United 0	1st Division	St. Mirren Park.
25/12/1915	Ayr United 2	Kilmarnock 0	1st Division	Somerset Park.
01/01/1916	Queen's Park 2	Ayr United 2	1st Division	Hampden Park.
03/01/1916	Ayr United 3	Dumbarton 1	1st Division	Somerset Park.
04/01/1916	Ayr United 2	Clyde 0	1st Division	Somerset Park.

188

08/01/1916	Ayr United 3	Hearts 1	1st Division	Somerset Park.
15/01/1916	Morton 0	Ayr United 1	1st Division	Cappielow Park.
22/01/1916	Ayr United 4	Queen's Park 1	1st Division	Somerset Park.
29/01/1916	Celtic 3	Ayr United 1	1st Division	Celtic Park.
05/02/1916	Ayr United 1	St. Mirren 1	1st Division	Somerset Park.
12/02/1916	Ayr United 2	Aberdeen 1	1st Division	Somerset Park.
19/02/1916	Raith Rovers 0	Ayr United 4	1st Division	Stark's Park.
26/02/1916	Ayr United 1	Rangers 0	1st Division	Somerset Park.
04/03/1916	Hamilton Accies 2	Ayr United 3	1st Division	Douglas Park.
11/03/1916	Ayr United 1	Dundee 2	1st Division	Somerset Park.
18/03/1916	Clyde 1	Ayr United 3	1st Division	Shawfield.
25/03/1916	Ayr United 6	Third Lanark 0	1st Division	Somerset Park.
01/04/1916	Partick Thistle 1	Ayr United 1	1st Division	Firhill Park.
08/04/1916	Ayr United 2	Airdrie 0	1st Division	Somerset Park.
15/04/1916	Motherwell 0	Ayr United 3	1st Division	Fir Park.
22/04/1916	Hibs 3	Ayr United 1	1st Division	Easter Road.
29/04/1916	Ayr United 4	Falkirk 1	1st Division	Somerset Park.
06/05/1916	Kilmarnock 1	Ayr United 2	Charity match for Kilmarnock Infirmary	Rugby Park.
13/05/1916	Ayr United 3	Queen's Park 1	Ayr Charity Cup final	Somerset Park.

Scottish League First Division

Played	Won	Drawn	Lost	For	Against	Points
38	20	8	10	72	45	48

Position fourth.

1916/17

12/08/1916	Ayr United 1	Rangers 3	Charity match for the Red Cross Society	Beresford Park.
19/08/1916	Ayr United 0	Third Lanark 1	1st Division	Somerset Park.
26/08/1916	Partick Thistle 3	Ayr United 0	1st Division	Firhill Park.
02/09/1916	Ayr United 0	Celtic 1	1st Division	Somerset Park.
09/09/1916	Kilmarnock 1	Ayr United 2	1st Division	Rugby Park.
16/09/1916	Ayr United 2	Hearts 0	1st Division	Somerset Park.
23/09/1916	Raith Rovers 1	Ayr United 3	1st Division	Stark's Park.
30/09/1916	Ayr United 1	Aberdeen 0	1st Division	Somerset Park.
07/10/1916	Ayr United 1	Rangers 3	1st Division	Somerset Park.
14/10/1916	Hibs 1	Ayr United 4	1st Division	Easter Road.
21/10/1916	Ayr United 1	Airdrie 1	1st Division	Somerset Park.
28/10/1916	St. Mirren 0	Ayr United 0	1st Division	St. Mirren Park.
04/11/1916	Ayr United 3	Dumbarton 1	1st Division	Somerset Park.
11/11/1916	Clyde 1	Ayr United 4	1st Division	Shawfield.
18/11/1916	Morton 2	Ayr United 0	1st Division	Cappielow Park.
25/11/1916	Ayr United 2	Hibs 1	1st Division	Somerset Park.
02/12/1916	Ayr United 0	Partick Thistle 0	1st Division	Somerset Park.
09/12/1916	Celtic 5	Ayr United 0	1st Division	Celtic Park.
16/12/1916	Ayr United 0	Kilmarnock 2	1st Division	Somerset Park.
23/12/1916	Hearts 1	Ayr United 2	1st Division	Tynecastle Park.
30/12/1916	Ayr United 1	Hamilton Accies 1	1st Division	Somerset Park.

Date	Match	Competition	Venue
01/01/1917	Queen's Park 3 Ayr United 2	1st Division	Hampden Park.
02/01/1917	Ayr United 2 Falkirk 2	1st Division	Somerset Park.
06/01/1917	Aberdeen 1 Ayr United 0	1st Division	Pittodrie.
13/01/1917	Ayr United 1 Motherwell 2	1st Division	Somerset Park.
20/01/1917	Dundee 2 Ayr United 1	1st Division	Dens Park.
27/01/1017	Motherwell 2 Ayr United 1	1st Division	Fir Park.
03/02/1917	Ayr United 1 Dundee 2	1st Division	Somerset Park.
10/02/1917	Rangers 1 Ayr United 0	1st Division	Ibrox Park.
17/02/1917	Ayr United 1 Clyde 1	1st Division	Somerset Park.
24/02/1917	Dumbarton 3 Ayr United 1	1st Division	Boghead Park.
03/03/1917	Ayr United 0 Morton 3	1st Division	Somerset Park.
10/03/1917	Falkirk 1 Ayr United 2	1st Division	Brockville Park.
17/03/1917	Ayr United 2 St. Mirren 1	1st Division	Somerset Park.
24/03/1917	Hamilton Accies 2 Ayr United 1	1st Division	Douglas Park.
31/03/1917	Third Lanark 4 Ayr United 3	1st Division	Cathkin Park.
07/04/1917	Ayr United 1 Queen's Park 1	1st Division	Somerset Park.
14/04/1917	Airdrie 1 Ayr United 0	1st Division	Broomfield Park.
21/04/1917	Ayr United 2 Raith Rovers 1	1st Division	Somerset Park.
28/04/1917	Ayr United 0 Kilmarnock 2	1st Division	Somerset Park.
26/05/1917	Ayr United 4 Stevenston United 2	Friendly For War Charities	Beresford Park.

Scottish League First Division

Played	Won	Drawn	Lost	For	Against	Points
38	12	7	19	47	59	31

Position fifteenth.

191

1917/18

11/08/1917	Ayr United 7	Ayr & District Junior Select 0	For Local Charities	Somerset Park.
18/08/1917	Celtic 4	Ayr United 0	1st Division	Celtic Park.
25/08/1917	Ayr United 2	Hamilton Accies 0	1st Division	Somerset Park.
01/09/1917	Kilmarnock 2	Ayr United 0	1st Division	Rugby Park.
08/09/1917	Ayr United 1	Airdrie 2	1st Division	Somerset Park.
15/09/1917	Third Lanark 1	Ayr United 1	1st Division	Cathkin Park.
22/09/1917	Ayr United 1	Clyde 3	1st Division	Somerset Park.
29/09/1917	Clydebank 3	Ayr United 1	1st Division	Clydeholm Park.
06/10/1917	St. Mirren 1	Ayr United 1	1st Division	St. Mirren Park.
13/10/1917	Ayr United 4	Falkirk 0	1st Division	Somerset Park.
20/10/1917	Hearts 2	Ayr United 0	1st Division	Tynecastle Park.
27/10/1917	Ayr United 2	Hibs 2	1st Division	Somerset Park.
03/11/1917	Rangers 0	Ayr United 0	1st Division	Ibrox Park.
10/11/1917	Ayr United 0	Dumbarton 1	1st Division	Somerset Park.
17/11/1917	Falkirk 3	Ayr United 0	1st Division	Brockville Park.
24/11/1917	Ayr United 0	Kilmarnock 3	1st Division	Somerset Park.
01/12/1917	Motherwell 5	Ayr United 1	1st Division	Fir Park.
08/12/1917	Ayr United 0	Morton 1	1st Division	Somerset Park.
15/12/1917	Ayr United 0	Partick Thistle 0	1st Division	Somerset Park.
22/12/1917	Airdrie 4	Ayr United 1	1st Division	Broomfield Park.
29/12/1917	Ayr United 1	Celtic 2	1st Division	Somerset Park.
01/01/1918	Queen's Park 0	Ayr United 0	1st Division	Hampden Park.

Date	Match	Competition	Venue
02/01/1918	Ayr United 4 Royal Flying Corps 2	Friendly.	Douglas Park.
05/01/1918	Hamilton Accies 0 Ayr United 3	1st Division	Somerset Park.
12/01/1918	Ayr United 2 St. Mirren 1	1st Division	Somerset Park.
26/01/1918	Ayr United 0 Rangers 2	1st Division	Somerset Park.
02/02/1918	Ayr United 2 Third Lanark 2	1st Division	Firhill Park.
09/02/1918	Partick Thistle 1 Ayr United 3	1st Division	Somerset Park.
16/02/1918	Ayr United 2 Queen's Park 3	1st Division	Somerset Park.
23/02/1918	Dumbarton 1 Ayr United 0	1st Division	Boghead Park.
02/03/1918	Ayr United 1 Motherwell 3	1st Division	Somerset Park.
09/03/1918	Ayr United 1 Clydebank 2	1st Division	Somerset Park.
16/03/1918	Falkirk 3 Ayr United 2	Friendly	Brockville Park.
23/03/1918	Ayr United 1 Hearts 1	1st Division	Somerset Park.
30/03/1918	Clyde 4 Ayr United 0	1st Division	Shawfield.
06/04/1918	Morton 1 Ayr United 0	1st Division	Cappielow Park.
13/04/1918	Queen's Park 2 Ayr United 1	Ayr Charity Cup final	Hampden Park.
20/04/1918	Hibs 1 Ayr United 1	1st Division	Easter Road.
27/04/1918	Ayr United 3 Kilmarnock 3	Friendly	Somerset Park.

Scottish League First Division

Played	Won	Drawn	Lost	For	Against	Points
34	5	9	20	32	61	19

Position bottom.

1918/19

17/08/1918	Ayr United 0	Third Lanark 2	1st Division	Somerset Park.
24/08/1918	St. Mirren 1	Ayr United 1	1st Division	St. Mirren Park.
31/08/1918	Ayr United 0	Partick Thistle 1	1st Division	Somerset Park.
07/09/1918	Celtic 1	Ayr United 0	1st Division	Celtic Park.
14/09/1918	Clyde 3	Ayr United 1	1st Division	Shawfield.
21/09/1918	Ayr United 1	Morton 5	1st Division	Somerset Park.
28/09/1918	Rangers 6	Ayr United 2	1st Division	Ibrox Park.
05/10/1918	Ayr United 1	Motherwell 2	1st Division	Somerset Park.
12/10/1918	Hearts 2	Ayr United 3	1st Division	Tynecastle Park.
19/10/1918	Ayr United 2	Queen's Park 0	1st Division	Somerset Park.
26/10/1918	Falkirk 4	Ayr United 4	1st Division	Brockville Park.
02/11/1918	Ayr United 5	Hibs 0	1st Division	Somerset Park.
09/11/1918	Ayr United 1	Airdrie 4	1st Division	Somerset Park.
16/11/1918	Kilmarnock 2	Ayr United 3	1st Division	Rugby Park.
23/11/1918	Ayr United 4	Hamilton Accies 1	1st Division	Somerset Park.
30/11/1918	Clydebank 1	Ayr United 3	1st Division	Clydeholm Park.
07/12/1918	Dumbarton 0	Ayr United 0	1st Division	Boghead Park.
14/12/1918	Ayr United 3	Kilmarnock 1	1st Division	Somerset Park.
21/12/1918	Airdrie 0	Ayr United 1	1st Division	Broomfield Park.
28/12/1918	Ayr United 5	Dumbarton 0	1st Division	Somerset Park.
01/01/1919	Queen's Park 2	Ayr United 2	1st Division	Hampden Park.
04/01/1919	Ayr United 1	Hearts 2	1st Division	Somerset Park.

194

Date	Result	Opponent	Competition	Venue
11/01/1919	Partick Thistle 1	Ayr United 3	1st Division	Firhill Park.
18/01/1919	Motherwell 4	Ayr United 0	1st Division	Fir Park.
25/01/1919	Ayr United 2	St. Mirren 0	1st Division	Somerset Park.
01/02/1919	Ayr United 2	Clydebank 0	1st Division	Somerset Park.
08/02/1919	Hamilton Accies 2	Ayr United 2	1st Division	Douglas Park.
15/02/1919	Ayr United 4	Clyde 1	1st Division	Somerset Park.
22/02/1919	Ayr United 2	Falkirk 0	1st Division	Somerset Park.
01/03/1919	Third Lanark 1	Ayr United 1	1st Division	Cathkin Park.
08/03/1919	Hibs 0	Ayr United 1	1st Division	Easter Road.
15/03/1919	Hibs 1	Ayr United 0	Victory Cup 2nd round	Easter Road.
22/03/1919	Ayr United 1	Rangers 1	1st Division	Somerset Park.
29/03/1919	Morton 1	Ayr United 1	1st Division	Cappielow Park.
05/04/1919	Ayr United 5	Renton 2	Friendly	Beresford Park.
19/04/1919	Kilmarnock 2	Ayr United 1	Friendly	Rugby Park.
26/04/1919	Ayr United 2	Kilmarnock 4	Friendly	Beresford Park.
03/05/1919	Ayr United 1	Vale of Leven 1	Friendly	Beresford Park.
10/05/1919	Ayr United 0	Celtic 2	1st Division	Somerset Park.
17/05/1919	Ayr United 4	Queen's Park 2	Ayr Charity Cup final	Somerset Park.

Scottish League First Division

Played	Won	Drawn	Lost	For	Against	Points
34	15	8	11	62	53	38
Position	sixth.					

1939/40 - first start

12/08/1939	Albion Rovers 5	Ayr United 0	1st Division	Cliftonhill Park.
19/08/1939	Ayr United 0	Rangers 4	1st Division	Somerset Park.
23/08/1939	Ayr United 2	Albion Rovers 1	1st Division	Somerset Park.
26/08/1939	Hearts 6	Ayr United 2	1st Division	Tynecastle Park.
30/08/1939	Kilmarnock 2	Ayr United 2	Ayrshire Cup (1938/39) final	Rugby Park.
02/09/1939	Ayr United 6	Hamilton Accies 1	1st Division	Somerset Park.

The First Division results were nullified and the programme was abandoned with Ayr United showing this record.

Played	Won	Drawn	Lost	For	Against	Points
5	2	0	3	10	17	4
Position	eighteenth.					

1939/40 Regional League

23/09/1939	Ayr United 3	Kilmarnock 1	Ayrshire Cup (1938/39) final replay	Somerset Park.
14/10/1939	Ayr United 2	Queen of the South 0	Scottish 2nd XI Cup 1st round	Somerset Park.

First teams were competing.

21/10/1939	Ayr United 0	Morton 1	Regional League	Somerset Park.
28/10/1939	Albion Rovers 2	Ayr United 1	Regional League	Cliftonhill Park.
04/11/1939	Ayr United 0	Rangers 2	Regional League	Somerset Park.
11/11/1939	Queen's Park 5	Ayr United 4	Regional League	Hampden Park.
18/11/1939	Ayr United 3	Clyde 2	Regional League	Somerset Park.
02/12/1939	Ayr United 7	Partick Thistle 0	Regional League	Somerset Park.
09/12/1939	Dumbarton 2	Ayr United 1	Regional League	Boghead Park.
16/12/1939	Ayr United 2	St. Mirren 3	Regional League	Somerset Park.
23/12/1939	Third Lanark 1	Ayr United 1	Regional League	Cathkin Park.
30/12/1939	Ayr United 2	Airdrie 1	Regional League	Somerset Park.
01/01/1940	Ayr United 2	Queen of the South 1	Regional League	Somerset Park.
02/01/1940	Kilmarnock 3	Ayr United 1	Regional League	Rugby Park.
06/01/1940	Motherwell 3	Ayr United 3	Regional League	Fir Park.
13/01/1940	Celtic 1	Ayr United 3	Regional League	Celtic Park.
10/02/1940	Ayr United 1	Queen's Park 2	Regional League	Somerset Park.
17/02/1940	Clyde 1	Ayr United 1	Regional League	Shawfield.
24/02/1940	Kilmarnock 1	Ayr United 0	Scottish Cup emergency competition 1st round, 1st leg	Rugby Park.
02/03/1940	Ayr United 2	Kilmarnock 2	Scottish Cup emergency competition, 1st round, 2nd leg	Somerset Park.

Date	Opponent	Competition	Venue
09/03/1940	Rangers 'A' 2 Ayr United 0	Friendly	Ibrox Park.
16/03/1940	St. Mirren 2 Ayr United 0	Regional League	St. Mirren Park.
23/03/1940	Ayr United 2 Third Lanark 4	Regional League	Somerset Park.
27/03/1940	Hamilton Accies 4 Ayr United 2	Regional League	Douglas Park.
30/03/1940	Airdrie 4 Ayr United 1	Regional League	Broomfield Park.
03/04/1940	Morton 4 Ayr United 1	Regional League	Cappielow Park.
06/04/1940	Queen of the South 3 Ayr United 0	Regional League	Palmerston Park.
10/04/1940	Ayr United 2 Albion Rovers 0	Regional League	Somerset Park.
13/04/1940	Ayr United 2 Kilmarnock 3	Regional League	Somerset Park.
15/04/1940	Kilmarnock 0 Ayr United 0	*Scottish 2nd XI Cup 3rd round	Rugby Park.
17/04/1940	Rangers 3 Ayr United 1	Regional League	Ibrox Park.
20/04/1940	Ayr United 0 Motherwell 1	Regional League	Somerset Park.
22/04/1940	Ayr United 3 Kilmarnock 0	*Scottish 2nd XI Cup 3rd round replay	Somerset Park.
24/04/1940	Ayr United 2 Hamilton Accies 2	Regional League	Somerset Park.
27/04/1940	Ayr United 1 Celtic 0	Regional League	Somerset Park.
01/05/1940	Partick Thistle 2 Ayr United 0	Regional League	Firhill Park.
08/05/1940	Ayr United 3 Celtic 0	*Scottish 2nd XI Cup semi-final	Somerset Park.
11/05/1940	Ayr United 4 Dumbarton 4	Regional League	Somerset Park.
25/05/1940	Aberdeen 1 Ayr United 1	*Scottish 2nd XI Cup final, 1st leg	Pittodrie.
01/06/1940	Ayr United 2 Aberdeen 1	*Scottish 2nd XI Cup final, 2nd leg	Somerset Park.

*First teams were competing.

Regional League

Played	Won	Drawn	Lost	For	Against	Points
30	7	5	8	50	66	19

Position fifteenth.

In lesser and better known conflicts they fell.

Index

1st Division 186, 187, 188, 189, 190, 191, 192, 193, 194, 195, 196
1st Gordon Highlanders 52
2nd Division 141, 142, 180, 181, 182, 183, 184, 185
2nd XI Association 168
3rd Glasgow Highlanders 62, 188
9th Holding Battalion 173
14th Argyll and Sutherland Highlanders 55
36th Division 170

A

Abercorn 5, 125, 180, 181, 182, 183, 184, 185
Aberdeen xiii, 10, 36, 62, 73, 80, 85, 89, 90, 98, 110, 121, 151, 155, 164, 166, 167, 168, 186, 187, 188, 189, 190, 191, 199
Afghanistan ix, xi, 175, 176
Africa xv, 77
Airdrie 29, 50, 63, 110, 121, 143, 151, 172, 180, 181, 182, 184, 185, 186, 187, 188, 189, 190, 191, 192, 193, 194, 198, 199
Air Raid Precautions Service 145, 166, 170, 172
Aitken, Andy 18, 131
Aitken Fraser 16
Aitken, Sam 141, 142, 143
Aitken, Sanny 40, 59
Albion Rovers 125, 147, 151, 196, 198, 199
Aldershot 70, 169
Aliens Restrictions Order 70
Allan (Third Lanark) 124
Alloa Athletic 59, 104, 151, 152, 160
Alston, Lieutenant 122
Annan 75
Annbank 110, 170, 180, 182, 183, 185
Antwerp 43
Anzacs 53
Arbroath 151
Ardennes 164
Ardiles, Ossie 131
Argyll and Sutherland Highlanders v, vii, 44, 55, 74, 75
Arras 124
Arsenal 93, 154
Arthurlie 184
Aston Villa 2
Athletic News 123
Attlee, Clement 173
Auld Kirk 103, 171
Austria 22, 52, 144
Ayr Academicals 19
Ayr Academy 25, 53
Ayr Advertiser 79, 88, 137, 139, 162, 167
Ayr and District Junior select 103
Ayr Barracks 27, 43, 128, 147
Ayr Burgh Tribunal 68, 71, 115
Ayr Cemetery xiv, 102
Ayr Charity Cup 21, 121, 125, 183, 185, 187, 189, 193, 195
Ayr County Council 145
Ayr Cricket Club 14, 78
Ayr FC vii, xi, 2, 3, 5, 7, 9, 10, 13, 18, 19, 21, 48, 57, 59, 91, 101, 116, 135, 138, 141, 142, 143, 180, 181, 182, 183, 184, 185
Ayr Fort 37
Ayr Gasworks 70
Ayr Guildry Cup 21
Ayr Harbour 71, 118, 126, 173,

201

Ayr Industrial School 37
Ayr Observer 1, 3, 4, 9, 79
Ayr Presbytery 81
Ayr Races 27, 28
Ayr Raiders 155
Ayr Schools Football Association 137
Ayr Sheriff Court 58, 71
Ayrshire Agricultural Association 78
Ayrshire and Galloway Hotel 5, 30
Ayrshire Appeals Tribunal 114
Ayrshire Cup 13, 14, 20, 34, 153, 180, 182, 183, 184, 196, 198
Ayrshire Dockyard 154, 169
Ayrshire Food Production Committee 113
Ayrshire League 103
Ayrshire Post 5, 9, 10, 19, 39, 48, 53, 65, 66, 68, 76, 79, 88, 105, 119, 120, 129, 142, 144, 157, 162, 170
Ayrshire Territorial Force Association 54
Ayrshire Yeomanry 5, 10, 29, 35, 43, 64, 65, 86, 153
Ayr Station 3, 27
Ayr Strollers 168
Ayr Thistle 17, 18, 19
Ayr Town Council 11, 12, 101, 113, 128, 170, 171, 172
Ayr Town Hall 122, 126
Ayr Tramways Committee 70
Ayr Tramways Depot 44
Ayr United i, iii, vii, ix, x, xi, xiii, xiv, xv, xvi, 2, 3, 16, 17, 19, 21, 27, 28, 29, 30, 32, 34, 35, 37, 40, 41, 44, 45, 46, 47, 48, 50, 54, 55, 57, 58, 59, 61, 62, 63, 65, 67, 68, 69, 70, 72, 73, 74, 75, 77, 78, 79, 80, 82, 83, 84, 85, 86, 87, 88, 89, 91, 92, 93, 94, 95, 96, 97, 98, 100, 103, 104, 105, 106, 107, 108, 109, 110, 111, 114, 116, 117, 118, 119, 120, 121, 122, 123, 124, 125, 129, 130, 134, 135, 136, 137, 138, 139, 140, 142, 143, 144, 145, 146, 147, 149, 151, 153, 154, 155, 156, 157, 158, 159, 160, 161, 162, 163, 165, 166, 167, 168, 169, 170, 171, 172, 173, 174, 175, 176, 177, 186, 187, 188, 189, 190, 191, 192, 193, 194, 195, 196, 198, 199

B

Baden-Powell, Robert 6
Ballantine Drive 16
Barr 161
Barrhill 161
Bathgate 111
Bathgate FC 41
Beale, William 87
Beaumont-Hamel v
Beckham, David ix, xiv, 176, 177
Beith 57, 124, 180, 184
Belfast 47, 132
Belgium 22, 25, 29, 64, 125, 164, 166, 175
Bell, John 40, 46, 63, 75, 77, 79, 81, 84, 86, 87, 110, 136
Bellringer, John vii, 28, 48, 55, 67, 74
Bennett, Alex 108, 109, 111, 134, 135, 136
Beresford Park 2, 4, 7, 8, 15, 20, 21, 28, 35, 37, 50, 62, 78, 98, 109, 142, 183, 185, 187, 188, 190, 191, 195
Beresford Terrace 16, 155
Berlin 22, 131, 132, 133, 149, 169, 171
Beveridge, William 53
Black Watch 57, 95
Blackburn Rovers 11, 48
Blacklands Park 183, 184
Blackpool 54

Blair, Tom 75
Bloomer, Steve 131, 133
Board of Agriculture 113, 114
Board of Trade 119
Boca Juniors 13
Boghead Park 34, 186, 188, 191, 193, 194, 198
Boning, James Marshall v
Boswell Park 81
Boulogne 166
Bowie, Douglas 147, 151, 172
Bowie, James 142, 151, 172
Boyd, James 41
Boys' Brigade 111
Bradford City 83
Brandfort Camp 14
Brazil 100, 101
Brechin City 152
Brentford 159
Brewster, George 110
Briggs, Alfie 41
Bristol 71
Bristol City 169
British Expeditionary Force 157, 167
Brock (Ayr United) 106, 110, 136
Brockville Park 109, 186, 188, 191, 192, 193, 194
Brodie, John 106, 138
Broomfield Park 180, 182, 185, 187, 188, 191, 193, 194, 199
Brown, Alec 18
Brown, Andrew 109
Brown, Sandy 132
Brown, Tom 162
Brownlie, Jimmy 70
Buchanan (Morton) 45
Buchanan (Archie) 143
Burma 170, 171
Burnfoothill Primrose 167
Burns Statue Square 8, 10, 27
Busby, Matt 170

C

Calais 166
Cameron, John xiv, 112, 119, 124, 131, 132, 133, 134, 143
Camp Bastion 176
Campbell, Archie vii, 34, 65, 124, 142
Campbell, Duncan 34
Campbell, Lieutenant 65
Camsell, George 93
Canadian Engineering Corps 34
Canadian Infantry 111
Capperauld, Robert vii, 55, 67, 74
Cappielow Park 67, 75, 180, 186, 188, 190, 193, 195, 199
Carmichael, Gabriel Baird v
Carrick Street Hall 138
Carroll, Tony 162, 168
Carsphairn 71
Cassidy, Joe 35, 40, 63, 70, 72, 138, 140
Cathkin Park 104, 186, 188, 191, 192, 195, 198
Catholic Young Men's Society of Scotland 137
Cavell, Edith 64
Celtic xiii, 34, 35, 37, 39, 48, 49, 63, 72, 73, 77, 80, 81, 91, 92, 103, 105, 106, 107, 108, 110, 111, 114, 116, 121, 135, 137, 138, 139, 142, 151, 160, 164, 168, 184, 186, 188, 189, 190, 192, 193, 194, 195, 198, 199
Celtic Park 72, 73, 86, 110, 159, 160, 186, 189, 190, 192, 194, 198
Chamberlain, Neville 145, 146, 150, 164
Chelsea 152
China 101, 163
Church Street 111, 131, 132
Churchill, Winston 47, 125, 164, 171
Clark, Jacky 149, 154, 159, 160, 161, 162, 163

Clark, James 43
Clifford, Tom vii, 91
Cliftonhill Park 196, 198
Clune Park 181, 182, 185
Clyde 35, 65, 69, 70, 77, 104, 105, 116, 121, 151, 154, 161, 162, 163, 182, 183, 184, 185, 187, 188, 189, 190, 191, 192, 193, 194, 195, 198
Clydebank 78, 86, 105, 106, 138, 150, 192, 193, 194, 195
Clydeholm Park 192, 194
Clydesdale Bank 20
Collingwood Battalion 62
Collins, Canon 139
Colmonell 161
Colville, John 151
Commandos 163
Connell, Andy ix, xiv, 175, 176
Copeland, David 132
Corbett, Alex 170, 173
Cowdenbeath 151
Cox, Jacky 147, 159
Coylton 18, 63
Craig (Ayr United) 146, 154
Craigmillar Buildings 13
Craik, Jimmy 154, 157, 159
Crinan Canal 75
Cringan, Willie 77, 106, 107, 110, 111, 140
Croall, James vii, 152
Crosbie, Johnny xiii, 26, 28, 29, 35, 43, 48, 50, 61, 75, 86, 104, 109, 136, 140
Crossan, Paddy 41
Cunard 132
Cupar 35, 43
Currie, Davy 146, 159, 160
Currie, Duncan 41
Czechoslovakia 145, 146

D

Dainty, Herbert 40, 44, 139
Daladier, Edouard 145
Dale, Athur 37, 48
Dam Park 16, 78
Dardanelles 53, 55, 57, 62, 63, 65, 67, 74
Darvel 18, 147
Dean, Dixie 93, 133
Defence of the Realm Act 58
Dens Park 43, 59, 139, 185, 186, 188, 191
Derby, Lord 64, 68
Devonport, Lord 92
Dimmer, Hyam 146, 162, 169
Distinguished Conduct Medal 111
Dodds, Joe 116
Douglas Park 181, 183, 184, 186, 189, 191, 193, 195, 199
Douglas Wanderers 182
Dowdles (Ayr FC) 91
Downing Street 150
Dresden FC 132
Drumley Colliery 114
Duff, Andrew 79
Dumbarton 34, 65, 85, 93, 110, 115, 121, 139, 151, 157, 172, 186, 188, 190, 191, 192, 193, 194, 198, 199
Dumfries 5, 6, 147, 162, 170
Duncan, George 105
Duncan, Rev. 41, 81, 105
Dundee 43, 44, 58, 59, 90, 93, 98, 121, 139, 151, 154, 185, 186, 187, 188, 189, 191
Dundee, City of 150
Dundee Hibs 139, 140
Dundee Tigers 155
Dundee United 151, 160
Dunfermline 150
Dunfermline Athletic 16, 151
Dunfermline Vikings 155
Dunkirk 167, 168
Dunlop, W. 68
Dunterlie Park 184
Dyer, Jimmy 146, 159, 160, 173
Dykes, Jimmy 167

E

Eadon, John 124
Easter Road 35, 116, 134, 186, 189, 190, 193, 195
East Fife 151
Easton, George 121
East Stirling 5, 152, 181, 182, 183, 185
Edinburgh 25, 39, 43, 116, 120, 150, 152
Educational Institute of Scotland 138
Elandslaagte 3
Elba Street 55
Ellis, Ernie 41
Elmbank 131
Epsom 52
Etaples Military Cemetery 117
Everton 59, 93, 95, 110, 132

F

Falkirk 41, 73, 95, 107, 109, 120, 121, 123, 151, 152, 159, 186, 187, 188, 189, 191, 192, 193, 194, 195
Falkirk Lions 155
Faubourg D'amiens Cemetery 124
Ferdinand, Franz 22
Ferguson, Alex 16
Ferguson, William 117, 134
Ferrier, Bob 172
Fife Flyers 155
Findlay, Norman 41
Firhill Park 48, 80, 187, 189, 190, 193, 195, 199
Fir Park 72, 180, 181, 183, 185, 187, 189, 191, 192, 195, 198
Firth of Clyde 163
Fish Cross 20, 171
Fisher, George Alfred 75
Flanders 43, 106, 107, 125
Food Committee 108, 113, 119
Football League 28, 54, 55, 72, 77, 93, 120, 134, 151

Forfar 167
Forfar Athletic 59, 93, 152
Forfarshire Association 152
Fort Matilda 53
Fort Street 27
France 22, 25, 39, 47, 51, 77, 78, 79, 86, 95, 98, 100, 104, 117, 125, 143, 157, 164, 175
French, John 35
Frew, James 41
Fulham 169
Fullarton, Alexander 17
Fullarton, Harry 17, 18
Fullarton, Harry junior 18

G

Gaffney, Sergeant 43
Galbraith, Curly 143
Gallagher, Patsy 37
Galloway, Captain 12
Galston 9, 20, 182, 184
Garden (Queen's Park) 142
Geddes, Auckland 119
Gemmell, David 146
Gemson, Alice 141
Gemson, Ann 141
Gemson, Anne 141
Gemson, George 137
Gemson, Lawrence ix, 51, 62, 98, 117, 121, 134, 137, 138, 139, 140, 141
German Ocean 70
Germany 22, 25, 35, 52, 70, 80, 89, 95, 100, 101, 106, 108, 116, 119, 126, 131, 133, 144, 145, 146, 149, 150, 157, 164, 175
Gestapo 144
Getgood, George 63, 81
Gillespie, Alex 142
Girvan 184
Glasgow 11, 12, 19, 20, 37, 44, 48, 54, 58, 101, 110, 120, 121, 122, 136, 137, 150, 159, 161, 162

Glasgow and South Western Railway Company 120
Glasgow Corporation 15
Glasgow Cup 34
Glenbuck 18, 29, 132, 136
Glenbuck Cherrypickers 86
Glossop 91
Godfrey, Peter 41
Godfrey, Robert 41
Goldie G. 75
Goldie J. 75
Goodwin, Hilly xiii, 40, 55, 56
Gordon Terrace 111
Gould (Celtic) 160
Gourlay, Jimmy 110
Govan 91, 141
Govan, David 146, 168
Govandale Park 180
Gracie, Thomas 41, 50
Graham, George 151
Graham, Harry 41
Gray, Alec xiii, 35, 36, 77, 80
Gray, Charles 50, 87, 97, 122
Gray, WC & Sons 55
Green, Michael ix, xiv, 177
Green's Stars 37
Greenock 11, 12, 44, 53, 67, 85, 160
Green's Picturedrome 81
Grimsby Town 48

H

Haddington 8
Haldane, Lord 46
Hall, Jimmy xiv, 146, 158, 159, 162
Hamilton Accies 2, 5, 103, 105, 111, 121, 147, 149, 150, 151, 167, 180, 181, 182, 183, 184, 186, 187, 188, 189, 190, 191, 192, 193, 194, 195, 196, 199
Hamilton, George 155, 157, 159, 167
Hamilton, Gladstone 142, 143
Hamilton, Jock 101
Hamilton, Thomas 75
Hampden Park 41, 65, 186, 188, 191, 193, 194, 198
Hammersmith 137
Harper, Bert 173
Hawkhill 180, 182, 184
Hay, Jimmy x, xiii, 75, 77, 90, 92, 106, 107, 110, 114, 115, 116, 135, 136, 140
Hazebrouck 125
Hearts 2, 34, 37, 39, 41, 48, 50, 62, 65, 73, 83, 88, 97, 107, 121, 122, 125, 145, 146, 151, 167, 186, 188, 190, 192, 193, 194, 196
Heberden, Mr 18
Helles Memorial 55
Henderson, David 173
Hennessey (Third Lanark) 110
Henry (Manchester City) 142
Herbertson, Sam vii, 55, 67, 74
Hess, Rudolf 144
Hibernian 21, 35, 45, 61, 85, 108, 116, 121, 126, 136, 139, 140, 151, 186, 187, 188, 189, 190, 192, 193, 194, 195
Highbury 154
Highland Light Infantry v, 143
Hill, Davie 34
Himmler, Heinrich 144
Hindenburg Line 125
Hiroshima 172
Hitler, Adolf 144, 145, 146
Holland 164, 166, 175
Holland Street School 152
Hood, John 48
Hourstons 86
Houston, James Blair 58
Huddersfield Town 164
Hungary 52
Hurlford 182
Hyslop (Celtic) 106, 138

I

Ibrox Park 18, 92, 108, 139, 185, 187, 188, 191, 192, 194, 199
Ingram, Cammie 75, 77, 86
Ireland 47, 132
Irish League 54
Irish Sea 47
Irvine 54, 147, 155, 170
Italy 52, 171

J

Jackson, Colonel 2
Jackson, John 72, 75, 77, 107
Jackson, Alex 168
Japan 172, 173
Jarrow 55
Jarvis (Stoke City) 142
Jerusalem 111
Jockey Club 27, 52
John Street 134
Johnston, Joe 5
Johnston, Maurice 135
Johnstone 142
Johnstone (Partick Thistle) 159
Jutland 75

K

Kaiser Wilhelm 25, 69, 130
Kandahar 175
Kelly, H. 44
Kelly, Jerry 93
Kelly, John 168
Kerr, Gordon 73, 77, 80, 81, 85, 89, 95
Kerr, Hugh vii, 116
Kerr, William vii, 124
Kidderminster 63
Kidderminster Harriers 64
Killan, Mark 18
Kilmarnock xiii, 3, 13, 19, 35, 65, 73, 74, 75, 82, 83, 87, 103, 104, 107, 109, 120, 121, 123, 129, 130, 135, 151, 161, 164, 182, 185, 186, 187, 188, 189, 190, 191, 192, 193, 194, 195, 196, 198, 199
Kilmarnock Infirmary 74, 189
Kilmarnock (Town) 20, 39, 54, 170, 175
Kilwinning 59
Kilwinning Eglinton 182, 183, 184, 185
Kimberley 10
Kingcase 5
King Edward 21
King's Park 151, 157
King Street 13, 173
Kinning Park 17
Kintyre Peninsula 163
Kirkcudbright 71
Kirkintilloch 125
Kirkland (Ayr United) 154
Kitchener, Lord 17, 46, 54, 76
Kruger, Paul 1, 5, 8

L

Ladysmith 10
Ladywell Park 185
La Kreule Military Cemetery 125
Lambeth 152
Lanarkshire Yeomanry 29, 43
Lancet, The 39
Lanham, Bailie 170
Largs 93
Law, Bonar 125
Lawton 169
Leeds City 48
Le Havre 46, 47
Leishman, James 41
Leitch, Jimmy 173
Leith 134
Leith Athletic 151, 152, 180, 182, 183, 184

Limbless Soldiers Fund 75
Lindsay, W. 143
Linthouse 91, 142, 180
Liverpool, City of 52
Liverpool 170
Lock, Herbert 104, 108, 136
Logan, Ruth 52
London 30, 34, 46, 63, 68, 71, 117, 151, 152
London Scottish vii, 117
Low Green 17, 19, 58, 171
Low, James 41
Luftwaffe 161
Lusitania 52, 64
Luton Town 91, 162
Luxembourg 164
Lyall, Jack xiii, 37, 38, 40, 44, 48, 55
Lyon J.C. 150
Lyon, Willie 160

Mac/Mc

Macaulay, Donald 46, 47
MacLean, John 58
MacLeod, Ally 16
McAndrew, William 151
McAtee, Andy 116
McBain, Neil xiv, 28, 48, 93, 94, 95, 125, 140
McBride, Hugh 57
McBride, John 57
McBride, Peter 18, 57
McCall, Andy xiv, 164, 165
McColl, R.S. 142, 143
McConnell, Hugh 154, 157, 159
McCrae, George 41, 43
McCrae's Battalion 41, 43
McDonald, Archie 48
McDonald, Hugh 11, 48
McDonald, John 11, 48
McDowall, John 31
McGibbons, Terry xiv, 147, 148, 154, 169

McInally, Tommy 106, 138
McKenzie, Alex 75, 77, 85
McLaughlan, Switcher xiii, 40, 59, 60, 75, 77, 103, 136, 142
McLean, Archie 101
McMenemy, Jimmy 142
McMenemy, John 142
McMillan, Archie 40
McNaughton (Ayr United) 105, 106, 136
McNeil, Norrie xiv, 174
McStay, Jock 138
McStay, Willie xiii, 40, 48, 49, 77, 107, 138, 140

M

Mafeking 6, 7, 8, 9
Maginot Line 164, 166
Main, Alan 59
Malcolm, John 173
Maley, Alec 106, 138
Maley, Charles 139
Maley, Tom 137, 138
Maley, Willie 106, 121, 137, 138
Malta 57, 63
Manchester City 55, 142, 155
Manchester United 16, 117, 170
Marshall, Jimmy (Great War) 85, 97, 107
Marshall, Jimmy (2nd World War) 146, 154, 162
Massie, Alex 2
Massie, Willie 2, 142
Massey, Lee 142
Mathie-Morton, John 128
Maybole 118, 161
Maybole FC 181, 185
Mayes, Jock 146
Meadowside 180, 185
Melvin, Jimmy 173
Mercer, Bob 41
Merchiston Park 181, 182, 185

Middlesbrough 93, 132, 142
Middleton, Billy xiv, 40, 55, 61, 64, 70, 81, 83, 86, 89, 93, 95, 98, 99, 104, 106, 109, 114, 116, 124, 136
Midton Road 16
Military Medal 110
Military Service Act 110
Military Service Bill 67, 68
Miller (Parkhouse) 142
Miller, Kenny 135
Miller Road 27
Mill Street 118
Ministry of National Service 119
Mitchell, John 103
Montgomery, W. 98, 107
Montrose 152
Moore, Bobby 131
Moore, Thomas 157
Morton xiii, 32, 34, 43, 44, 45, 50, 66, 67, 75, 85, 93, 110, 121, 139, 151, 154, 160, 180, 181, 186, 188, 190, 191, 192, 193, 194, 195, 198, 199
Motherwell 5, 72, 73, 90, 91, 110, 115, 121, 151, 159, 172, 180, 181, 182, 183, 185, 187, 188, 189, 191, 192, 193, 194, 195, 198, 199
Murray, Harry 62, 63
Murray, J.S. 151
Murray, David, 168
Mussolini, Benito 145

N

Nagasaki 172
Naismith, Doctor 13
Neilson, P. 110
Ness, Annan 41
Nevin, Jack 40, 63, 95
Newall, Jock 154, 157, 159, 167
Newall, Tom 167
Newcastle 55

Newcastle United 18, 45, 114, 131
New Cumnock 71
Newmarket 52
Newfield 142
Newfoundlanders xiv, 102, 103
Newfoundland Regiment 101, 103
Newton 7, 11, 17, 35, 46, 78, 126
Newton Heath 117
Newton Rovers 169
New York 52
New Zealand 53, 167
Nisbet, George xiv, 96, 97, 104, 107
Normandy 153
Northampton Town 155
North Sea 70
Nottingham Forest 91, 164

O

O'Kane, Joe 81
Old Racecourse 16, 113, 114
Orange Free State 1
Orion 10, 182
Orkney Islands 76
Oswald Road 143
Ottawa 111
Output of Beer (Restriction) Act 90

P

Paisley 65
Palmer (Raith Rovers) 83
Palmers of Jarrow 55
Parkhouse vii, xi, 2, 3, 4, 5, 6, 7, 13, 18, 19, 20, 21, 30, 34, 124, 131, 132, 138, 142, 143, 152, 184
Partick Thistle 2, 4, 27, 29, 40, 47, 48, 73, 80, 110, 121, 151, 159, 180, 184, 185, 186, 187, 188, 189, 190, 192, 193, 194, 195, 198, 199
Passchendaele 111
Patrick, Millar 11, 15, 16
Pattillo, Jock 168

209

Pebble Park 180, 182
Pele 131
Pentland, Fred 132
Perth Panthers 155
Petershill 107
Phillips, Charlie 86, 143
Pilcher's Column 14
Pittodrie 167, 187, 188, 191, 199
Players' Union 132
Plumstead 117
Poland 146, 149
Porteous, David v
Port Glasgow 53
Port Glasgow Athletic 180, 182, 185
Powderhall 154, 183
Preston 137, 139
Preston North End 18, 57, 139, 147, 154
Preston, Robert, 41
Prestwick 35, 129
Princip, Gavrilo 22

Q

Queen of the South 151, 155, 162, 163, 164, 198, 199
Queen's Park 17, 21, 41, 48, 50, 65, 66, 97, 121, 122, 125, 132, 142, 151, 186, 187, 188, 189, 191, 193, 194, 195, 198
Queen's Park Rangers 48
Queen Victoria xvi, 10, 16, 17

R

Raith Rovers 5, 41, 43, 72, 83, 95, 97, 121, 139, 142, 151, 181, 186, 187, 188, 189, 190, 191
Raitt (Third Lanark) 142
Ralston Park 180, 181, 183, 184
Rangers xiii, 17, 37, 39, 42, 78, 92, 104, 107, 108, 121, 135, 136, 139, 142, 151, 152, 155, 163, 168, 186, 187, 188, 189, 190, 191, 192, 193, 194, 195, 196, 198, 199
Rankinston 91
Reading 63, 72
Red Army 169, 171
Red Cross 30, 35, 59, 78, 190
Regional League xi, 154, 155, 163, 164, 198, 199
Renfrew Juniors 124
Renfrewshire 75, 150
Renton 195
Rhineland 145
Riccarton 129
Richardson, Jimmy xiii, xiv, 28, 35, 37, 40, 42, 43, 50, 55, 62, 77, 95, 104, 125, 127, 140
Rifle Brigade 136
River Plate 13
Riverside Park 9, 182
Robbsland Park 16, 17
Roberts, Lord 4
Roberts (Queen's Park) 142
Robertson, John 160
Robertson, Tommy 154, 155, 159, 161, 162
Rodger, Fally 155, 159, 160, 168
Rome 141
Rose, Shamrock and Thistle, The 137
Ross (Ayr United) 146
Royal Air Force 111, 122, 157, 159, 169, 175
Royal Artillery xiv, 90, 115, 153
Royal Engineers 93, 159, 167
Royal Field Artillery vii, 75, 125
Royal Flying Corps 105, 109, 111, 193
Royal Scots Fusiliers vii, 14, 27, 43, 45, 47, 53, 55, 57, 68, 73, 74, 83, 91, 124, 128
Rugby Park 13, 35, 73, 129, 162, 182, 183, 186, 188, 189, 190, 192, 194, 195, 196, 198, 199
Ruhleben 131, 132

Russia 22, 76
Rutherglen Glencairn 135, 149, 159

S

St.Bernard's 116, 151, 152, 182, 183, 184
St. Columba's Church 16
St. Crispin Works 118
St. John's All Stars 103
St. John's Daily Star 103
St. Johnstone 151, 164
St. Leonard's Road 16
St. Margaret's Church 139
St. Margaret's School 137
St. Mary's College 137
St. Mary's Catholic School 137
St. Mirren xvi, 10, 41, 65, 75, 78, 84, 95, 107, 111, 113, 121, 135, 151, 162, 181, 183, 186, 187, 188, 189, 190, 191, 192, 193, 194, 195, 198, 199
St. Quentin 11
Sandgate 126, 128
Sarajevo 22
Scotland 2, 18, 33, 34, 41, 53, 55, 58, 59, 62, 75, 84, 93, 106, 110, 114, 132, 135, 140, 142, 149, 150, 152, 160, 162, 168
Scott (Hearts) 41
Scottish 2nd xi Cup 35, 164, 166, 168, 198, 199
Scottish Command 169
Scottish County League 5, 181, 182
Scottish Cup 10, 17, 18, 34, 100, 135, 140, 152, 154, 182, 183, 185
Scottish Cup Emergency Competition 161, 198
Scottish Football Association 30, 33, 34, 72, 74, 87, 93, 100, 118, 121, 147, 150, 151, 161, 172
Scottish Football League 5, 28, 54, 72, 77, 89, 93, 105, 107, 120, 122, 123, 141, 150, 151, 161, 181, 183, 185, 187, 189, 191, 193, 195
Scottish Junior Football Association 93, 151
Scottish Qualifying Cup 9, 100, 117, 180, 182, 184
Serbia 22
Seymour, Stan 45
Shankland, Robert 111
Shankly, Alex 86, 105, 136
Shankly, Bill 86
Shankly, Bob 86
Shawfield 69, 116, 161, 183, 185, 189, 190, 193, 194, 198
Sheffield Wednesday 55
Sherwood Foresters 37
Simpson, Harry 57
Smith, Bob 160
Smith, Henry 59
Smith, Nick 18,
Smith, Peter 154, 173
Smith, S.W. 173
Sneddon, William 159, 160
Solway Firth 75
Somerset Park ix, xiii, xv, 2, 3, 6, 7, 12, 13, 15, 19, 23, 29, 35, 37, 39, 40, 50, 52, 55, 61, 70, 73, 75, 78, 84, 87, 91, 103, 105, 107, 108, 116, 136, 139, 141, 142, 143, 146, 147, 150, 151, 153, 155, 162, 169, 170, 172, 176, 180, 181, 182, 183, 184, 185, 186, 187, 188, 189, 190, 191, 192, 193, 194, 195, 196, 198, 199
Somerset Road ix, 129, 140, 141
Somerville, Archie 109, 136
Somme vii, xv, 41, 57, 76, 81, 89, 115, 123
South Africa 1, 2, 4, 5, 14, 15, 18
Southampton 59
Southern League 54, 77, 132, 134
South Harbour Street 173
South Petherton 152
Spence, Billy 4, 5
Spion Kop 13

211

Springvale Park 16
S.S. and E. [Scottish Stamping and Engineering] Athletic 169
Stark's Park 181, 187, 189, 190
Steen, Tom 30, 51, 87, 121, 146, 151
Stenhousemuir 151, 182
Stevenston Thistle 13, 183
Stevenston United 98, 191
Stewart, Albert 154, 173
Stewart, Alex 154
Stobhill Hospital 35
Strain (Ayr United) 146
Stranraer 4
Submarine Service 95
Sudetenland 145
Summers, Eddie 159
Sunday Mail 149
Sunderland 77, 110
Swansea Town 159

T

Tait, Sandy 132
Tam's Brig 130
Taylor, A.J.P. 25
Taylor, Jock 146
Templeton, Bobby 18
Templeton, Thomas 19
Templeton, James and Son 118
Tennant, H.J. 33
Third Lanark 4, 34, 45, 70, 79, 104, 109, 110, 116, 121, 124, 142, 151, 186, 187, 188, 189, 190, 191, 192, 193, 194, 195, 198, 199
Thompson, Frank xiv, 156, 157, 159
Thomson, John 138
Thomson (Hamilton Accies) 167
Thow, Lewis 159, 167
Tottenham Hotspur 124, 132, 134
Transvaal 1, 3, 5
Trinity United Free Church 11, 16
Troon 35
Troup, Alec 59, 93, 95, 107

Tryfield Place 52
Turkey 55, 67
Turnberry 109
Turner, Donald 159
Tynecastle Park 41, 62, 88, 125, 186, 188, 190, 192, 194, 196

U

U-boats 52, 70, 85, 101
United States of America 95
Ure, Ian 53

V

Vale of Leven 17, 18, 195
Verdun 69, 70, 71, 72, 89
Victoria Cross 3, 4, 111
Victory Cup 195
VE Day 171, 173
VJ Day 173
Voluntary Park 169
Von Richtofen, Baron 116

W

Waddell, George xiii, 82, 83, 107
Waggon Road 173
Waaikraal 18
Wales 53, 71
Walker W.G. 78
Wallace Tower 20, 128
Wallacetown 7, 11, 17, 78, 111
War Office 30, 31, 33, 34, 51, 52, 53
Washington DC 52
Wattie, Henry 41
Webb (Ayr United) 107
Wellington Lane 17
Welsh (Raith Rovers) 83
Westerlea 116
Western Command 169
Western Front vii, 44, 48, 89, 91, 100, 104, 105, 115, 119, 123, 126

Western League 169
Western Race Meeting 35
West of Scotland Catholic
    Teachers' Association 138
White, Archie 142
White Hart Lane 134
White, Sprigger 48, 80, 85, 89,
    97, 98
Whiteford, Jock 154, 159, 161, 173
Whitletts Road 140
Whitletts Victoria 169
Wilson, Willie 41
Winnipeg 111
Woolwich 48
Woolwich Arsenal 11, 48
Wolves 64, 110
Wright, Andrew 146, 168
Wright, Billy 169

Y

Yardley, Jimmy 146
Yeovil vii
Y.M.C.A. Hall 50
Ypres 53, 72
Yule, Thomas 107